the shadow that seeks the sun

a story about yogis, bhogis,
and an unexpected encounter

ray brooks

tellwell

Editor: Luci Yamamoto, www.luciyamamoto.com
Cover concept and design: Dianne Brooks

Front cover photograph by Ray Brooks: The River Ganges
covering the bottom flagstone step on the *ghats*
Interior photographs: Ray Brooks and Dianne Brooks

Email: tststs@shaw.ca
Website: raybrooks.org

Tellwell Talent
www.tellwell.ca

ISBN
978-1-988186-37-5 (Paperback)
978-1-988186-36-8 (eBook)

This is a true story. We have changed the names of some of the people described in *The Shadow that Seeks the Sun* out of respect for their privacy.

Also by Ray Brooks

Blowing Zen: *Finding an Authentic Life*
First published by H.J. Kramer /
New World Library, San Francisco, CA., U.S.A. 2000
Ich ging den Weg der Zen-Flöte, Ansata Verlag, Germany,
German Edition - Published 2000

Blowing Zen - Republished, Revised and Expanded Edition
Sentient Publications, Boulder, CO., U.S.A. 2011

CD Zen Shakuhachi, Imagine Records,
Quebec, Canada 1995

CD Hollow Bell, New Albion Records
San Francisco, U.S.A. 2000

with deep affection and gratitude

Rudra
John Mirra
Usha Devi

Table of Contents

talks with rudra

acknowledgments

Heartfelt thanks to the cast of characters appearing as Dianne Brooks, co-writer and frontline editor. Luci Yamamoto, for her guidance, expertise and professionalism in editing and shaping the manuscript. Kaan Mertol for his technical skills in recovering the project from cyber-space. Ron McGeary for his patience and contribution to the graphics layout for the 'first draft' book cover. Debra Johnson for proofreading several of the chapters and giving feedback at an early stage. Siddhartha Krishna for his generous help when called upon. Alan Neachall and Sara Daly for reading the manuscript and giving feedback and encouragement. Sarah Pollard for her help on first few chapters at an early stage. Chris Lea for pointing us in the direction of Rishikesh. Timothy Conway for introducing us to Tat Wale baba. Erin Ball, Production Manager and Jordan Mitchell, Graphic Designer at Tellwell Talent, Inc. Francis Lucille, Rupert Spira, Ambika Shah Chhabra, Sandy Neyle, Ray Shahan, and all of our good friends at the Hall of Mirrors and in Rishikesh.

This is a small section of the Muni Ki Reti *ghats* on the banks of the River Ganges in Rishikesh, Uttarakhand, India. "Ghats" is a recurring word used throughout the book and describes a series of steps leading down to a river, particularly a holy river that is used for ritual bathing. In the distance is Ram Jhula, a suspension bridge.

Dianne Brooks
Co-writer
The Shadow that Seeks the Sun

The Shadow that Seeks the Sun
(the title is a metaphor pointing to the imagined
separate self that seeks its true nature.)

chapter one

Yogis and Bhogis

Rishikesh: 2007

"I am God. Give me one hundred rupees!"

An ash-smeared sadhu stood in front of me, his brass pot thrust under my nose.

"You must be kidding, baba."

"Yes sir, he said, wobbling his head. I am not kidding."

With a dismissive flick of my hand, I stepped out of his way and walked on.

"Fifty rupees, sir!"

I kept walking.

"Ten rupees!" God yelled his final offer.

The fruit seller, delighted with the show, called after me, "One rupee days are over, sir."

1

The local street vendors in Rishikesh call men like God "money babas" or "bhogis." They claim that they are not true holy men, just beggars or even criminals on the run. With so many foreigners visiting this small pilgrimage town, it has become a very lucrative area for babas who like to prey on the naiveté of "spiritual" tourists. If you spent any time on the ghats, it's easy to identify true sadhus by the way they conduct themselves. "True sadhus" live by the will of God, never beg, and accept money or food only if it is offered. They tend to stay away from the busy tourist areas during the day, preferring to spend their time in contemplation and meditation. And those renunciates who live in the forest will come down to the river before sunrise to perform their *pūjā*[1] rituals. You would never see a bhogi taking a holy dip in the Ganga at four a.m.

As the clock tower at Parmarth Ashram solemnly struck nine, the morning sun was burning off the last of the river mist. Hundreds of cormorants sat on the boulders in the shallow part of the river and more were landing. As the birds settled, they spread their wings and warmed their bodies.

Another ashram decided it was nine o'clock and manually banged out an irregular beat. In the distance, I could hear more

---

1   Pūjā is the act of making a spiritual connection with the "Divine," and it can be performed through invocation, prayer, song, or ritual.

bells counting out the time. There wasn't a clock in India that was right.

The "Monkey Punky Gang," as Dianne has named a small group of the local children, trotted towards me grinning playfully and chattering away with one another. They wore woolen hats that looked like tea cozies, ill-fitting sweaters full of holes, long ragged skirts and baggy trousers that covered their skinny legs. Some wore flip-flops; others, plastic shoes two sizes too big. There would be no school for them today. Today, and most days, they were the flower sellers responsible for the small flower bowls that people floated down the river as offerings to Mother Ganga.

"Sachin!" they screamed when they spotted me. They ran over to see if I had anything for them.

"Flaaawar Sachin?"

"No flower," I said.

"Please, Sachin," they begged, jostling one another for my business.

The secret to a peaceful life on the ghats, especially if staying a long time, is to avoid buying offerings from the children. If you bought from one, you had to buy from all. I often saw Westerners realizing their dream of meditating on the banks of the sacred Ganga, only to be swamped by children who insisted that they buy an offering. Unless you were firm and told them to clear off, they would never leave you alone.

One of the children spotted the ferry coming. The gang waved goodbye and dashed off to terrorize the passengers.

"Good morning!"

I looked in the direction of the greeting and recognized a man I'd met on the ferry the previous day. It was early morning, and the small boat that crossed the River Ganges between Muni Ki Reti and Swag Ashram was just pulling out. He'd seen me running to the dock and had called out to the helmsman, who yelled for me to wait as he maneuvered the boat back to the rickety jetty. With an outstretched arm, the ticket collector grabbed my hand as I jumped across the rapidly widening gap between dry land and the boat. What a relief. I'd just spent weeks searching for a flute teacher who could show me some of the classical India *raga* on my *shakuhachi*,[2] and definitely didn't want to be late for my first lesson.

Among the few passengers making the crossing, most were wrapped in ragged cloth and blankets, hunched against the cold wind blowing down from the Himalayas. The man who had shouted for the boat to stop was sitting across from me, and he acknowledged my thanks with a nod and a smile. He was a distinguished-looking man, conspicuously free of the religious paraphernalia so ubiquitous around here. I guessed that he must be of Anglo-Indian descent because of his light

---

2   Japanese bamboo flute.

skin and unusual blue eyes. He was remarkably well dressed and I couldn't help but admire his style. He wore a well-cut, collarless navy-blue jacket—the type made popular by India's post-independence Prime Minister Jawaharlal Nehru in the late 1940s—and a beautifully made burgundy pashmina scarf. Despite his silver-grey hair, it was hard to say how old he was— sixty, perhaps, or a well-preserved seventy.

As customary when crossing this sacred river, the sadhu sitting on my right, dressed in a faded saffron robe, brought his palms together at his forehead and bellowed a blessing to Mother Ganga: "Om Nama Shivaya!" He then leaned over the side of the boat, scooped a handful of water, and threw it over his head, most of it splashing on mine.

"Thanks *baba*! That should bring me good health in the New Year," I said, wiping the water from my face. The distinguished man laughed and said, "Not if it goes in your mouth it won't."

The sadhu grinned at me and then uttered more prayers before he took another scoop and drank it.

A sadhu sitting to my left yelled "Jai Shri Ram!" and then tossed a palm full of the purifying elixir over his head, drenching me again.

"It's wise to keep one's mouth tightly shut when crossing this river," the distinguished man said with an accent that was more British than Indian. He seemed to be finding it all very amusing.

"Yes, sacred or not, that's good advice. Works quite well on land, too."

"All rivers are sacred," he said, "but sadly this one is not sacred enough to drink from these days."

The old Rajasthani pilgrim next to him leaned over the side of the boat and began filling a large plastic container. His tiny wife, withered from a life of hardship in the desert, was talking incessantly about the sacred "*paani*," as her husband stretched farther and farther toward the water. Within a second he screamed as the weight of the bottle pulled his skinny body from his seat and wrenched the half-full container from his hand. The Anglo-Indian man instantly reached out and grabbed a handful of his clothes to keep the poor man from falling overboard.

"That was close," I said, noting his quick reactions.

The ferry landed with a bump. I said goodbye to my travel companion and hurried off to my lesson. I didn't expect to see him again.

"Ah, good morning," I said and walked up the steps towards him. "I see you've found the best bench in all of Northern India." The view across the river encompassed many prestigious ashrams and small hermitages. The giant *Shiva*[3] statue

---

3   Hindu God: Shiva, the destroyer, is one of three powerful mythological deities. He is responsible for the destruction of our imperfections to ensure our spiritual progress. (*Brahma* is the creator and *Vishnu*, the preserver.)

at Parmarth tilted, half submerged in the blue-green, glacial-melt water.

"The monsoon flooding dragged poor Shiva off his pedestal again this year," I said, admiring the impact the great "creator and destroyer" made.

"Yes, indeed it did. Lord Shiva is not having much luck at Parmarth. Maybe he should find himself a new ashram."

"It's true. This must be the third time he's tried to leave in as many years."

"Your name is Sachin?" he asked, apparently surprised that a foreigner would have an Indian name.

"No, only the children call me Sachin, after the cricketer. I sometimes play cricket with them on the ghats, though they don't let me bat any more. I've hit a couple of lucky sixes into the river, which means they have to go all the way to the Bay of Bengal to get their ball back."

"Ah, the great Sachin Tendulkar!"

"Yes. Not so bad being named after an Indian cricket god, wouldn't you say? My real name is Ray, by the way."

"Nice to meet you, Ray. I'm Rudra." We shook hands.

"Are you visiting Rishikesh, Rudra?"

"No, I sometimes stay here during the winter months. But my home is up in Mussoorie."

"Oh, whereabouts?"

"A little village to the east of the mall, called Sister's Bazaar. Do you know it?"

Giant statue of Lord Shiva at Parmarth Ashram
before the monsoon destroyed it

"Yes, I know it well. My wife and I had hoped to make that area home base during the winter, but we discovered that it was much too cold for us."

"Yes, February in particular can be quite bitter. I'd ask you to sit, Ray, but it's getting a little warm here. I usually move closer to the water at this time of day."

He stood and asked which way I was going. I was going to Dayananda Ashram. He was heading in the same direction and invited me to walk with him.

I can tell by your accent that you're from England," he said. "What part are you from?"

"I was born in Newcastle but moved to London when I was 16."

"I've never been to Newcastle but I lived in London in my twenties, in a place called Holborn."

"I know Holborn. What were you doing there?"

"My parents packed me off to university after I graduated from school."

As we walked along the ghats, I noticed Om Prakash, the owner of Shanti's Restaurant, and waved. He was standing at the water's edge and had just finished his morning pūjā, offering Mother Ganga her daily class of milk.

"How long have you been coming here, Ray?"

"To Rishikesh? For quite a few years. And to India, probably for more than twenty-five years by now. I return with my wife nearly every winter."

"How marvelous."

"Yes, we love it, but I must say it gets harder and harder to cope with all the traffic and motorbikes these days. We're always on the lookout for a new base. Somewhere quieter. India feels like it's becoming a little crazier every year."

"Yes, it's certainly changing fast."

"Mostly for the better, though. I was in and out of the bank yesterday in ten minutes!"

"Yes, I know what you mean. I just booked a train ticket to Delhi online. Marvelous stuff."

"Back in the eighties, my record for waiting in a bank was two hours. I remember one time, in Almora, I was trying to persuade the clerk to cash my traveler's checks when the fuse board on the wall burst into flames. All the lights went out, the room filled with smoke, and the place broke into pandemonium. The security guard rushed over with a bucket of sand in one hand and his shotgun in the other. I thought he was going to give me the bucket, but instead he handed me the gun and started throwing the sand onto the fuse box. The good ol' days."

"The gun probably wasn't loaded anyway," Rudra said, laughing.

We reached the spot where he liked to sit. I was familiar with this section of the ghats, which had been partially damaged by floods last year.

"This is probably the quietest spot along this side of the river," he said, as he removed his jacket. "Please, feel free to join me, if you're not in a hurry."

I was enjoying his company and decided to accept his invitation.

We made ourselves comfortable a couple of steps up from the waters edge. The bottom flagstone step was submerged in the river and had turned a deep pinkish-red color. The sound of rushing water filled my ears, demanding a few moments of silence. A garland of marigolds and red rose petals floated by, followed by another garland, a plastic bag, and a lone flip-flop.

"May I ask, Ray? Why the fascination with India for so many years?"

I stalled for a moment and smiled, remembering my childhood. I couldn't tell him it all began with a knock on my grandmother's front door. . .

"I'll be there in a minute, Terry!"

Another knock came, much louder.

"Jesus, Terry, you're early!" I shouted as I pulled open the door. "Oh, sorry mister!" I stared in amazement. The man standing there was not Terry and he was certainly not from around here; miners never wore clothes like his unless they were going to a fancy dress party. Wrapped around his head was a canary-yellow length of cloth, framing a shining brown face, a thick black beard, and a moustache that curled at its

11

edges. He was wearing a tweed blazer, a lime-green shirt, and a bright purple tie, and, in his arms, he held an open a suitcase full of more colorful ties.

"Is your mother in, sonny boy?" he asked, speaking with the strangest accent I had ever heard. I didn't respond. I was hypnotized by the sight of him and his ties.

"Is your mother at home, son?"

I shook my head. "I live with my granma." Unable to resist, I reached out and touched a tomato-red tie, rubbing it between my fingers.

"They're a bit bright for my granddad, mister."

"That's pure Indian silk, sonny boy, the finest money can buy. Tell your grandmother I'll call again."

Off he went to the next house. I grabbed my football, slammed the door, and followed him, remaining at a distance all the way along the row of terraced houses. Each time he glanced back at me, I turned the other away and dribbled my ball. When a neighbor's door opened, I had a good stare at him. One woman asked where he was from.

"Newcastle, madam," he said.

"No man, yer silly bugga. Where yer really from?"

"India, madam."

"India! Eee, you're a long way from home, pet."

I followed him all the way to the bus stop and stood next to him while he waited. When the bus arrived, he turned to

me and said, "I'm very glad to have met you today, sonny boy."
Then he shook my hand and said goodbye.

That night, when Grandad returned from his shift at the pit.
I blurted out every detail about my new friend in the strange
yellow hat. He was in a good mood and laughed at my enthu-
siasm. "Hold your horses will yer, Kemosabe. I've just come
through the bloody door." Granma handed him a mug of tea
and said there was a bucket of hot water waiting for him in
the scullery.

Later that evening Grandad showed me a map in our old
world atlas. "That's India, lad." It was exactly the same shape as
the damp patch on my bedroom ceiling. He told me that India
was once part of the great British Empire. The way Grandad
pronounced the word "India" carried me to a faraway land,
teeming with mysterious people who wore colorful hats and
neckties. I decided then and there that I wanted to go to India
when I grew up.

". . . Well, my fascination with India goes back a long way,
Rudra. What brings my wife, Dianne, and me back every year is
our love of the mountains and the rural areas of Northern India,
and—the old British Raj connection has always intrigued us.
I'm also very interested in Indian philosophy, which is a big
part of the attraction for me. It's a funny relationship, I feel
so frustrated here at times, but the beauty and chaos of India

13

offer incredible magic moments that I haven't experienced anywhere else."

"Yes, I've heard this said about India. The contrasts can be quite intense here, can't they?"

There was a long pause and again the sound of water filled my ears.

"Ray, you mentioned that you were on your way to Dayananda Ashram."

"Yes. I go most days. At this time of year Swami Dayananda is away in Southern India, so the ashram is virtually empty. It's a quiet place to sit without being disturbed. I like the library there too, so I often go and read in the afternoon."

"Are you interested in any particular teachings, Ray, or just Indian philosophy in general?"

"Well, at first, I studied Zen philosophy, but over the years my studies have led me to the traditional Advaita[4] non-duality teachings. I've also studied some of the lesser known Indian teachers as well."

He began to laugh. "There are certainly plenty of those to choose from here. Is Swami Dayananda your teacher?"

"No. But I've read several of his books. I would say the nearest I've ever come to having a teacher was Jiddu Krishnamurti. Are you familiar with his work?"

---

4   A vedantic doctrine that identifies the individual self (Ātman) with the ground of reality (Brahman).

"Yes. I've read a couple of his books and I saw him speak once in Chennai—of course, it was Madras in those days. He liked to put the cat amongst the pigeons, didn't he?"

"That's what I liked about him. I attended his talks in California many years ago and managed to get a private meeting with him just before he died."

"You met him? How wonderful. I always liked the way he challenged organized religion and our Indian gurus."

"Yes, me too. I heard that the CIA investigated him at one point during the sixties but found he was 'only talking,' so he wasn't seen as a threat to the U.S. I also read somewhere that he was called 'the guru's guru.'"

"The guru's guru. You couldn't get a better title than that, could you? Krishnamurti might have been seen as a threat if they had understood what he was trying to convey. He spoke of a revolution, but not the kind that would interest the CIA."

"He definitely challenged our beliefs, didn't he? He seemed to speak without any fear."

"Yes, that's exactly right. He spoke from direct experience, and in that, there is no fear." He paused for a moment and held my gaze.

"So, did you find Krishnamurti's teachings helpful, Ray?"

"Yes, to some degree. He became an important influence in my life, and his teachings have made a difference to how I see things. I discovered him at a time when I was starting to question the way I was living. Even though I didn't fully understand

15

everything he was saying, I felt he was speaking the truth, and I stuck with him for many years. But, I'm still trying to understand the deeper meaning of what he said, and grasp his 'observer is the observed' teaching.

"So you haven't finished searching, Ray?"

"Are we ever finished searching, Rudra? It seems like everyone is searching for some sort of meaning. Don't you think?"

"Well, it certainly appears that way. Everyone longs and looks for happiness. You see this fellow coming towards us. He longs for freedom, which is really just another word for peace and happiness."

His gaze was directed towards a man walking along the water's edge. He had long silver hair and was dressed in white all except for a pair of bright purple gloves.

"In the Hindu religion he is what we call a Muni. He has taken a vow of silence. It's his method of finding liberation."

Rudra waved to him and a purple hand waved back.

We sat quietly and watched an osprey circle and swoop over the river. This is what I loved about being in India—the vibrancy, the unexpected, the chance encounters, the conversations that quickly moved from small talk into the question of life and death.

Talk One

"It's funny, I feel such an exquisite sense of freedom just sitting here next to the Ganga talking with you, Rudra. This qualifies as one of those magic moments I was telling you about. If there was nothing more than this, it would be enough."

"You know, Ray. . ." He hesitated, perhaps unsure whether to carry on. ". . . heightened experiences only have significance if they point to what is already here."

"Well, I've always felt that they point to something beyond the ordinary. I doubt if I'd be sitting here with you today if it weren't for these experiences. More than likely, I'd be caught up in the system, living the whole 'catastrophe.' They've motivated me to make changes, to keep going, to keep discovering more about myself."

Rudra nodded unconvincingly and looked out across the river. Undeterred, I carried on.

"I'd like to think these experiences have brought me to this point, Rudra. It was a heightened experience that changed the direction of my life, many years ago."

"Ray..." He hesitated again. This time there was a long pause before he spoke. "Ray, is any of what you've just said true?"

I was startled by the directness of his question.

"You see, there are no 'experiences.' There is *only* experience. For there to be experiences there would have to be 'someone' to have them. For there to be someone, the knowing and the known would have to be separate. If you're really interested in the truth you have to see this."

"I know what you're referring to, but that has never been my experience. I'm certain that what I'm looking for is connected to these experiences. They've shown me that there's more to life than the mundane and that there is the possibility of freedom."

"Whether you recognize it or not, you have never been apart from experience. Have you ever experienced a time when there wasn't experience? If you have. How would you know? Ray, what you're looking for is not found in experiences. What you're looking for is beyond the very idea of freedom itself and not in future 'experiences.' If we don't remain open and aware of what these 'experiences' are directly pointing to, it's easy to be carried away by them and to make the mistake of believing yourself to be something perceived—something separate from that which is already present. Without seeing this clearly, and based on what you've said, you will always be searching for freedom in some future experience and missing the obvious."

"The obvious? What is the obvious that I'm missing, Rudra?"

"*This*, Ray. The last place you look—your *actual experience*, which is right here. This changeless experience is so familiar, so obvious that it goes unnoticed. As for 'experiences' bringing you to this point, how could anything bring you to where you have never left, or could ever leave? No matter how sublime the experience, it only ever points to *this*, where you already are."

I looked away, unable to stand the scrutiny of his gaze any longer.

"Stop resisting what you're hearing for a moment, Ray, and look at your experience right now. What do you find?"

"What I find is you and I talking together sitting by the river."

"I wasn't asking you for a story about what is apparently going on. Close your eyes and look. What do you find?"

Without giving a description, I was unsure how to answer.

"Well, just me."

"Yes, just the experience of what you normally refer to as you? So you find only experience, right?"

"I just want to be clear what you mean by the word 'experience,' Rudra."

"What it feels like to be you—beingness."

"Okay. . . Yes, then just experience."

"You can find only being, yes?"

19

". . . Yes, just being."

"Irrefutable *being* that needs no proof—aware-beingness, that proves all else. Is there any effort required to know this beingness?"

"Well, no. None at all."

"Right, there's no effort or special conditions for it to *be*. It is so obvious that it is disregarded and believed to be a by-product of the brain or some kind of higher power. When I used the word 'obvious,' Ray, I wasn't being condescending in any way. I'm referring to that which you have just seen clearly without any effort. That which is closer than close, yet totally overlooked. Just experience, as you are, and not what thought says that you are, or should be."

"So you're suggesting that these heightened experiences that I've had get in the way of finding the obvious?"

"You don't have to find the obvious. You *are* the obvious. And what is stopping you from discovering this is the idea that being is not present and is found in some future experience. You're only a glance away from seeing this for yourself. Why not trust your actual experience instead of trusting your beliefs?"

"But Rudra, the freedom during these experiences is unmistakable. If the clue to this freedom isn't in our experiences, where else could it possibly be?"

"Ray, you've just seen where it is. Where else could it be? All that keeps you from seeing this is the common belief that 'someone' is having an experience. You and experience are not two things. There is only ever experience. Sorry, I'm already making it sound too complicated. It's much simpler than words can express."

I could hardly believe the direction our conversation was taking. Apart from Krishnamurti, I had never met anyone who spoke with such insight and certainty. He was so open and at ease, and there was not a trace of preaching in his voice. I felt exhilarated in his company and was definitely in no hurry to leave.

"I can see you're very interested in all of this, Ray. But as long as you believe that you are separate and independent from experience—that there is an inside self and an outside world—I can assure you that you'll be like a dog chasing its own tail."

"Ever since meeting Krishnamurti, intellectually, I have always known that the separation between the 'experiencer' and the 'experience' is the very root of the problem, but, in actuality, this has never become clear to me."

"And it will never become clear as long as you believe you are looking from the point of view of an experiencer—a separate self."

"Who or what is it that knows that 'I' and 'experience' are not separate?"

"That which is hearing this voice; the simple knowing of this current experience, without interpretation. All that you know of yourself, beyond any doubt, is that you are self-aware."

21

I'd been sitting for almost an hour and the stone step was beginning to feel uncomfortably hard. I took off my jacket and sat on it. Rudra seemed to realize that I needed time to digest what he was saying and paused for several minutes.

"When you see clearly that there is only one 'knowing,' one timeless experience of *this*, what could possibly trouble you but imagination?" He paused. "Ray, we're entering territory that will take more than a few minutes to explore. Do you have time to continue?"

"Yes, I have plenty of time."

"All right. If I may ask, Ray, where do you find yourself when these magic moments come to an end?"

"Good question. . . Well, it's as if I have one foot in the past and one foot in the future. Longing for something—'becoming' might be a good word to describe it. A feeling of being unsettled might sum it up."

"Unsettled, yes. Wanting things to be different. Is that sense of not being complete with you now?"

"Now? No. Not at all. I'm really enjoying our talk and there's an experience of wellbeing. I'm just here. I'm present and I'm aware. I couldn't think of a better place to be."

"Be careful here. Present and aware are not two separate things. Presence-awareness is the experience of beingness itself. So, yes, there is just experience—the indescribable certainty that you exist. When I use the word 'experience,' I am not referring to experiences in time, but only the awareness of 'now,' which are one and the same."

"I'm more familiar with using the word 'awareness' in these types of conversations. Are you using 'experience' as a synonym for 'awareness.'"

"Yes. Awareness is just another name for experience. The meaning of awareness can be misunderstood and abstract, where experience is known by all. So, Ray, when you look now, there is only the certainty of experience—this aware-beingness. There's not a sense of becoming or wanting a more pleasurable experience."

"Yes, that's right. There's just aware-beingness."

"Have you ever known a time when you were not this aware-beingness?"

"Well, there are moments when I'm busy and I forget that I'm aware, or when I'm lost in thought and off in a dream world."

"For thought to be at all, surely awareness must be there. You would have to be present for thought to arise, wouldn't you? If not—if something has existence outside of aware-ness—it would have to be a belief, wouldn't it?"

Although somewhat mystified, I was fully absorbed by his words. Rudra could see that I was grappling with his statements and kept quiet again for a moment.

"Ray, 'experience' or 'awareness' or whatever you want to call it, are just other names for 'you.' That is, the simple sense of 'I.'"

"I've always thought 'I' was the problem."

"We are not talking about the 'I' belief that comes with a story of past and future. I'm referring to the simple experience of 'I' that is complete and perfect. Beingness itself."

"If beingness is already complete, why does it leave perfection and go in search of a better state? That seems to be all it ever does."

"You never leave perfection to go on a search. There's not two of you; one looking for another. Thought appears unauthored, just like any other appearance, creating the illusion of separation. Once this seamless oneness divides into entities—mind, objects, and world—the divisions seem very real. Then thought goes on an endless path, searching for a self that has never been lost. It's a futile path. Like a shadow that seeks the sun."

Rudra paused and stared across the river.

"Ray, there is only ever *this*—this present moment—and it is all you. Without *you*, *awareness,* nothing could possibly be."

I looked at the scene around me. The sun illuminated the pink walls of the ashram across the river. About one hundred yards to my left, a pack of dogs were barking and fighting over something snatched from the remains of a smoldering funeral pyre. A songbird alighted on a nearby rock, shook its feathers, bobbed its tiny body, and began to sing with startling volume and beauty.

"As I said, Rudra, apart from a few glimpses, I understand what you're saying only conceptually. I've tried so hard, for so long, to see this. In truth, there's something I'm just not getting."

"Something *thought* is not getting—thought cannot get this. Thought cannot know peace. It can only know *about* peace. Ray, it sounds as if you simply want to move from where you are to where you want to be. That new place is peace and happiness. Is this true?"

For a moment, the beauty of the bird's song overpowered his question. I looked at Rudra and then back at the bird, but it was gone.

"Yes," I said, a little disappointed with my answer. "As you've said, Rudra, everyone is looking for peace and happiness."

"Ray, peace is not somewhere else. Peace is no other than the absence of resistance to what 'is.' It is your ever-present nature, the light of aware-presence. It could never cease to shine. The difficulty lies in explaining its utter simplicity."

Rudra's words were firm but the timbre of his voice never changed and his expression remained calm. The Muni paraded past us again on what must have been his fifth lap. We didn't speak for a few minutes.

"Ray, I'm sorry, I'd really like to stay longer, but I must attend to some business in town."

"Yes, of course, Rudra. I hope I haven't kept you?"

"No, I have enough time to get there. Such a pleasure talking to you this morning. I hope our conversation has been helpful in some way."

"It has. Would it be possible to meet again?"

"Yes, of course. I can't tomorrow, but how about on Wednesday at the same time?"

"I'll be here."

We stood up and Rudra placed his palms together.

"Ray, these magic moments are quite wonderful, but words cannot describe the beauty and the love of simply being. To be here, in this love, is easy. All else is effort. *Namaste.*"

chapter two

Awakening to the Dream

London: Thirty years earlier

It was turning into a great night out. I was feeling carefree and happy to be in such lively company. On nights like this, the questioning was not there. The gnawing sense of anxiety and emptiness, so familiar I believed it was normal, was concealed beneath banter, rounds of drinks, and celebration of the Christmas holiday.

My local pub, The Ship, attracted a great crowd of people. It was only a couple of doors from the famous Marquee Club on Wardour Street. Musicians who were playing at the Marquee usually started out with a few drinks at The Ship before going onstage.

It was Boxing Day 1976. George Best, one of the greatest footballers of all time and an idol of mine, was standing at the bar. George had recently ended his career with Manchester United and was now playing for second division Fulham Football Club. George was with keyboardist Alan Price and bassist Chas Chandler of The Animals and another flamboyant Fulham footballer named Rodney Marsh. My friends and I had gone to Stamford Bridge that afternoon to see the London Derby between Chelsea and Fulham. I used this as a pretense to go over and say hello. George and the lads were welcoming, which might have had something to do with my buying them a round of drinks. They didn't seem bothered that they'd been beaten 2-0 by Chelsea. The barman handed back my change from a twenty and, since they were all in good spirits, I asked them for their autographs.

"George, would you mind signing this?" I said, handing him a crisp five-pound note. A pen emerged from somewhere and he signed it, followed by the others. Like me, Alan Price and Chas Chandler were born in Newcastle in the northeast of England, and recognizing my accent, Chas asked what area I was from. I told him it was a small mining village called West Allotment. He knew it well and said he had played at the West Allotment Miners Club way back when he was too young to drink. Chas and I broke away from the main group to chat about Newcastle United Football Club and reminisce about the early sixties when The Animals were just starting out.

We talked about Jimi Hendrix, whom Chas had managed up until two years before Jimi's death in 1970. I told him that I'd seen Hendrix perform live at the Isle of Wight Festival, and he shared a few inside stories with me. Apparently it had been his idea to get Hendrix to set his guitar ablaze on that infamous night at the London Astoria in 1967. "Jimi was going to finish the set with the song 'Fire,' and I had this great idea to pour lighter fluid on his Stratocaster and get him to throw a match to it. The flames shot into the air and burned Jimi's hands. Lucky for me he was able to finish the set."

Chas bought me a drink and when it was my shout, I bought him one back—with the five-pound note signed by all of them.

I'd arranged a date with a woman I'd met a week ago and left the pub just before last orders to meet her at Samantha's nightclub. The place was packed when I got there, but I managed to find my date and get a couple of seats at the bar. We ordered drinks and I tried my best to follow her conversation over the loud music and all the revelers shouting to one another.

Twenty minutes into our chat, a sudden and strong sensation came over me. It felt as if the whole place had gone quiet, like sound was at a distance. Overcome by the experience, I could neither ignore it nor shake it off. I tried to concentrate but kept losing the gist of what my date was talking about. I offered her another drink hoping the sound of my voice would return me to normal. But the sense of disassociation only expanded. I could see her lips moving but I'd lost all contact with the meaning of the words. I felt like a spectator outside of my body, watching actors in a play. I was fully cognizant of the "dream" that was taking place, but I was not a part of it. Overwhelmed, I mumbled that I felt unwell and told my confused date that I had to leave. She looked concerned and offered to drive me home. I refused and apologized for spoiling the evening. Without waiting for a response, I pushed through the crowd in search of oxygen.

I wandered through the backstreets of London's West End. When I reached Marble Arch, I crossed to Speakers' Corner and entered the blackness of Hyde Park. I hesitated for a moment and then walked until I came to a familiar area not far from the Serpentine River. The last time I was here, in this very spot, I was with my ex-wife, seven years earlier on July 5th, 1969. Hundreds of people had gathered to see the Rolling Stones memorial concert for Brian Jones.

I stood motionless, listening to the speeding traffic on Park Lane and gazing at the surrounding crown of city lights. The sense of detachment had not receded. I walked down to the lake and sat on a damp wooden bench. The disassociation had turned into a sense of spaciousness now and a feeling of wellbeing devoid of the usual emptiness. Whatever this was, I didn't want it to end.

Eventually, I made my way towards Hyde Park Gate and onto Kensington High Street and walked the four miles home.

By the time I climbed into bed, the intensity of the experience was fading. I made an effort to hang onto it until I fell into a shallow sleep.

When I awoke the next morning, the experience was gone. The whole day, I thought about what had happened and how I might get the feeling back.

This event marked my first few days off work in weeks. I'd been installing complex electrical systems into The National Art Gallery and in the underground vaults of the Bank of England. I loved my work, but it was demanding; I had to be there at night while the buildings were closed to the public. The pressure of the job may well have been the catalyst for what had happened in the nightclub. It didn't seem to matter how or why it had occurred, only that I had experienced a tremendous sense of freedom, maybe even fulfillment. For many years, my life had lacked meaning; the experience that night left me with a feeling that the future held great promise.

When I told my friends what had happened, they suggested that I'd had a break from reality. They cracked jokes and renamed me Cosmic Ray.

"Cosmic Ray said he couldn't make it to the pub last night. Said he was staying in to meditate. Still, it's better than sitting around doing nothing!"

My friend Cleggy, in one of his more philosophical moments, decided that I was having an "existential" crisis.

31

"To be or not to be. Forget it, mate! No one knows the answer. I feel like that most mornings, but it soon passes. It's all bollocks, Ray. You've just got to get on with the cards you've been dealt. You've been dealt a good hand, mate."

It was hard to take myself seriously when my friends were trying to wind me up all the time, especially when they were mercilessly good at it. They loved their ruthless humor as much as they loved their nights out and joked that this meaning of life stuff might be a good way to impress women. Cleggy said women loved all that sensitive talk.

In the end, we put the incident down to overwork and exhaustion—nothing a few pints of personality with the lads couldn't sort out. To them, anything bordering on the "spiritual" was for hippies and LSD freaks. They were good at managing their anxiety and fear and definitely did not want anything to upset the status quo. It was as if we were all sleepwalking from hangover to hangover, only now I kept waking up and questioning the way I was living. It wasn't a comfortable feeling. But I felt like I had no choice.

Over the next few months, as I became engrossed in exploring what might have happened that night, I saw less and less of my friends. We called one another, but I could tell they were not as enthusiastic about asking me to meet up. Maybe they sensed that I, too, was pulling away.

****

London was losing its charm for me, so I began looking into the possibility of moving to the countryside. My job was the only consideration. I wondered whether it would be possible to commute to the city every day. I didn't want to give my position up; I couldn't imagine better or more interesting work. Each assignment was different and most of the job locations were steeped in London's long and fascinating history. One day I would be checking the humidity in the Tate Gallery and the next, maintaining the electrical systems at the Houses of Parliament or Westminster Abbey. After a couple of test drives from London to the small town of Reigate in Surrey, I decided that the commute was workable. It took about four months to complete the move and sublet my London flat.

****

The next year was a mixture of highs and lows. I was full of discontent, disillusionment, and insecurity but, at times, I had a taste of clarity, even joy. I had already cut down on alcohol and now stopped drinking altogether. I joined a sports club and new people began to appear in my life. I'd even taken an interest in cooking healthy food at home, which was a complete change from eating take-away curries and pie and chips in pubs.

I'd get the occasional call from my friend Ronnie. No doubt I had unsettled him. Although he never admitted it, he was interested in hearing about my new life. He told me he often woke up in the middle of the night, feeling that there must be more to existence than the way he was living. Ronnie invited me up to London one Sunday to an art exhibition. I wasn't sure if he was taking the piss out of me; the name of the exhibition was "Man in Conflict." He mentioned free drinks and food and added that a few of the lads would be there.

I almost didn't go. I'd been driving back and forth to London all week and parking in the city was always a problem on weekends. By the time I arrived, the gallery was crowded with well-dressed people mingling in small groups around the paintings. I declined the glass of wine I was offered and made my way to an extravagant buffet table. If my friends were there, they'd be near the wine and food and not wandering about looking at paintings. I didn't recognize anyone, but did notice a young woman who was talking with a group. I couldn't take my eyes off her. She wore her hair almost to her waist and was casually, if a bit untidily, dressed for the occasion in tight jeans tucked into high-heeled boots. She was laughing and had a vivacious, easy energy about her. She saw me looking and immediately invited me to join the group. She asked my name and then introduced me to her friends. We spent the rest of the evening chatting and ended up taking a long walk along the Thames Embankment. This walk marked the beginning of thousands of miles of walking together, all over the world.

Dianne was naturally free spirited, full of adventure, and unlike anyone I had met before. Our relationship developed quickly and, as we became closer, I told her what had happened at Samantha's and how it had been a catalyst for change. She didn't seem surprised. Dianne practiced yoga and told me that reports of this kind weren't uncommon in spiritual literature, especially in Indian yoga philosophy. But she agreed with my friends that the experience had probably been catalyzed by stress and overwork.

Most days, on my lunch break, I searched the bookshops in Charing Cross Road. I picked up a few self-help paperbacks that focused on things like "personal growth" or developing "the self," but they didn't get at what I was looking for, even though I really had no idea what I was looking for. Eventually, I found myself in the philosophy section at Watkins Books in Russell Square, scanning the spines for a title I might understand. I settled on one called simply *Classical Indian Philosophy*, which I bought and read with great interest, although without much understanding. The book seemed complicated and exotic, but I did discover a description of an experience similar to mine, which the author had described as "oneness." The explanation of oneness provided some clues to what might have occurred. A particular paragraph caught my attention: it referred to a non-separation between subject and object, leading to a state of oneness. That summed up—as close as I could get—what had happened.

I began to read about Zen and Indian philosophy and even some books by Christian mystics and poets.

The owner of my local bookshop in Reigate noticed my buying many titles on Eastern philosophy and recommended an Indian teacher named Jiddu Krishnamurti. He showed me a speech Krishnamurti had made in 1929 to thousands of his followers when he resigned as head of the Order of the Star. Krishnamurti had literally given up his role as the coming "world teacher" and the head of the organization. The speech had a huge impact on me.

I maintain that Truth is a pathless land, and you cannot approach it by any path whatsoever, by any religion, by any sect. That is my point of view and I adhere to it unconditionally. Truth being limitless, unconditioned, unapproachable by any path whatsoever, cannot be organized; nor should any organization be formed to lead or coerce people along a particular path. If you first understand that, then you will see how impossible it is to organize a belief...[5]

Krishnamurti's words resonated with me. I wasn't interested in abdicating my self-reliance by following a *guru* or joining a religion or sect. The speech was long and basically told his followers that they were on their own. Neither he, nor anyone else, could take them to truth, although he did seem to suggest that truth could be pointed to. The first Krishnamurti book I

---

5   For the full speech go to www.krishnamurti.org.

bought was *You are the World.* It was a difficult read, quite intellectual, and I sensed that Krishnamurti was saying something extremely important. I couldn't put it down. He spoke of being free of all belief and fear; of the urgency of finding out if there is a timeless state. A timeless state. The more I thought about this, the more it summed up my Hyde Park experience.

"*Can we live in freedom without conflict?*" This question captivated me. From what I could understand, Krishnamurti was suggesting that one could not come to this freedom, stillness, and peace through any practice or discipline, or by following any guru. That resonated with me. I wrote out a paragraph from *You are the World* and carried it around in my wallet until it was faded and illegible.

The world lies in yourself and if you know how to look, the key is in your hands. Nobody, no guru, no teacher, or practice, could give either the key or the door to open, except yourself.

After *You are the World*, I consumed as many books by Krishnamurti as I could find. The bookshop owner lent me his copy of *Freedom from the Known.* He told me that Krishnamurti was still alive—and that he gave weeklong public talks throughout the year in England, India, Switzerland, and California.

Hungry to understand more, I telephoned the Krishnamurti Foundation in the UK. When and where would his next series of talks take place? I had missed his gathering in England, but he would be speaking in Ojai, California, in two weeks.

I took a leave from work, bought a ticket to Los Angeles, and flew to California.

chapter three

K

I was never going to make it on time for Krishnamurti's first talk. I didn't have a clue where Ojai was, never mind Oak Grove School. The taxi from the airport in Los Angeles cost almost as much as my monthly mortgage payment and my driver, once in Ojai, kept asking for directions. Finally, we found Besant Road—more dirt track than road—and I was dropped off at a five-bar gate with less than ten minutes to spare. Beyond the gate, I could see a crowd of several hundred already settled on chairs and on the grass awaiting Krishnamurti's arrival. Only the crows squabbling high in the magnificent oaks broke the silence. I wasn't the only one cutting it fine. I caught up with two men ahead of me and walked behind them, feeling a bit less conspicuous. As we passed through the gate, I heard one of them say, "I'll go and move the car, K." It was Krishnamurti.

39

With a polite wave of his hand, he ushered me ahead. For a moment, I was transfixed by the sheer sight of the man. Here I was, in the United States of America, standing next to Krishnamurti. The next thing I knew, I was speaking to him. In the quiet of the grove I could hear my voice amplified in my ears.

"Excuse me, sir. Sorry to trouble you. I've come all the way from England to attend the talks, and I'm wondering if it would it be possible to have a private meeting with you?"

He didn't smile or skip a beat. "Certainly, sir. My secretary takes care of my appointments. If you would kindly speak to her, I'm sure it can be arranged."

He sounded more English than I did. I thanked him and then, feeling a little self-conscious, walked ahead of him into the Oak Grove. I found a place at the back of the audience and sat on my duffle bag. I promised myself that I'd be early for the next talk—and sit up front.

Krishnamurti stepped onto the raised platform and sat down on a simple wooden folding chair. He tucked his hands under his thighs and then looked around at the hushed crowd for several minutes. A few times, he seemed to stop and stare at someone he recognized. Only the crows remained unaffected by his presence.

"Don't you have anything better to do on this marvelous sunny day? Wouldn't you like to go for a picnic?" He paused and waited to see if anyone would take him up on his offer.

"What the speaker has to say requires your *complete* attention. If you are not completely serious, you are wasting your time here. The speaker doesn't care if you're here or not."

Ten minutes into the talk, Krishnamurti asked if we understood what the speaker was saying. Again, he paused for what felt like an eternity.

"Never mind, let's carry on. I'm not speaking to you anyway, with all of your noisy thoughts. I'm speaking to something much deeper. Maybe we'll plant a seed that will germinate and grow."

I couldn't hear clearly from so far back, so I made my way to the side of the crowd, closer to the stage.

"*Who* are you?" he asked, as he panned the audience. "*What* are you?" He waited, allowing us to consider his questions. In the pause, a voice from the crowd said, "Sir, could you tell us who you are and what you are?" Even the crows were quiet now. Krishnamurti's reply was swift and directed to the audience as a whole.

"Are you just curious about who the speaker is? Look, I am nobody. Simple as that. And if I tell you who the speaker is, what does it matter? How will that help you? You look and say, 'What a great man. I'm going to follow him. I'm going to imitate him—the way he walks, the way he talks, the way he looks, or whatever it is. I'm going to imitate him and take on his beliefs.' This is the pattern of the mind, you see. The Enlightened. The Guru. The Priest. The Teacher. You imitate them. Don't you see how absurdly silly this is? How childish this is? Don't you see the danger of imitation in following and believing? You are the result of all this. Your priests and your gurus don't actually say imitate me. They say follow me, follow this way, meditate or whatever and you will be enlightened or saved, or go to heaven and all that other nonsense—which is imitation, is it not? They give you no more than knowledge, and knowledge can never be new. You are living from the menu of life, constantly talking about the food that you'll get when you find the restaurant. In every aspect you imitate. Whatever you are—whether you're a Communist, Conservative, Catholic, Hindu or peace-loving hippie—you imitate. You become a believer and you join a club or a group. You have faith in another, who has said they will get you to where you want to be, only if you believe, only if you have faith. Has it worked for you? Look at the world today. Has what you're doing to this marvelous world worked?"

Again, he stopped, looking around at the intent faces in the audience.

"You've tried everything and it hasn't worked. Don't you see where division has led you? Don't you see that there can be no end to all of the violence, if you *imitate*? Conformity leads to violence. To be something other than what you are is the cause of all your problems."

It felt like Krishnamurti was speaking directly to me. Everything that I thought I was, I had cloned from those around me. I was shaped by the society and culture I grew up in—same ideals, same vision. I could understand what he was saying: Imitation leads to the battlefield; belief and conformity, to war.

"So, to find out who you are, not who the speaker is, is far more important, isn't it? To find out what you are, you have to look, you have to inquire to see if you are in any way separate from the inquirer, from the world. If you really see that, it gives tremendous vitality . . . beauty . . . love. You are no longer a small entity struggling in a corner of the earth. You *are* the world."

Krishnamurti looked around the crowd as if he felt great sorrow and compassion for us.

After the talk, the audience sat mesmerized in the stillness his words had created. There was no doubt; I had to meet this man.

A few people stood up and that was my cue to book my appointment. I mingled with Krishnamurti's entourage, which appeared to be a well-heeled and intellectual group. I recognized Krishnamurti's driver. Upon telling him of my short conversation with Krishnamurti, he walked me to an elegant European woman and introduced her as Krishnamurti's secretary. Before she recorded any of my details, she introduced me to those around her, including Mark Lee, president of the

Krishnamurti Foundation of America (KFA). She scheduled our meeting for five p.m. the next day.

The group graciously included me in their conversation and asked how I had discovered Krishnamurti. I learned that many of the people who attended the talks had been doing so for decades, following Krishnamurti from one venue to the next, all over the world. I could understand the attraction, but wondered why they followed him, considering the thrust of Krishnamurti's message about not following *any* authority or guru and being a light unto oneself. One Australian couple said they liked to travel to all of the Krishnamurti camps because the locations are so beautiful. Another man said he was taking every opportunity offered to listen to one of the most provocative and thought-provoking speakers while he was still with us. Krishnamurti was 83 years old then.

A member of the group asked if I needed a lift to where I was staying. "Thanks, but I'm staying within walking distance," I said. I'd tried to book accommodations before I left London, but all of the hotels in Ojai had been booked months in advance. So I brought a sleeping bag and ground sheet. I would sleep under the stars.

My meeting with Krishnamurti set, I said goodbye to my new friends and went in search of a decent spot for the night. Fortunately, the weather was great and I found a meadow with soft turf just a ten-minute's walk from the Oak Grove. I could hide my bag during the day in a thick stand of bamboo nearby.

I hitched my way into the small town of Ojai and was directed by one of the locals to a small deli.

While waiting in line, I chatted with a middle-aged man called George who was also attending the talks. I joined him at his table. For over twenty years George had followed Krishnamurti all the way to Europe and once to India. He said he hadn't seen me on the K circuit before, but had spotted me talking to the KFA president and the secretary. He was curious to know who I was. "Nobody," I said, disappointing him. George laughed and said I was already guilty of imitation. I explained that this was my first talk and that I had only just met the KFA people. Then I let him fill me in on the Krishnamurti gossip. I asked him why he thought people kept coming each year to hear Krishnamurti say the same things again and again.

"To find out what his secret is," George said. "We want to know how he can stay so clear while we struggle with the ups and downs of life."

George appeared to be quite open, so I asked if the talks he had attended over the years had had any lasting effect on him.

"There have been some changes in me but, as Krishnamurti would say, change is no change at all. I'm like a bee buzzing around the honey pot—so close."

He stopped speaking for a moment and carefully, with the side of his hand, brushed the crumbs on the table into his empty soup bowl. "You know," he said, laughing, "I could probably sit on that platform and give a talk about freedom and the observer and the observed and even get a bit of a following."

He spoke passionately and I could see how hard he was trying to understand Krishnamurti's message. I asked George if he had ever had a private meeting with him.

"Yes, many times over the years. Once I asked him straight out. "What is the secret, K? Why, after hearing you for so many years, am I not free? Why are you free while I am not?"

George seemed to want to stop there, but I prompted him to continue. Did you receive an answer?

"Yes, although it wasn't much help. K simply said, 'I don't mind what happens.'"

"Just that?"

"No. He said, 'When you live as this awareness, this sensitivity, life has an astonishing way of taking care of you. No matter what is happening, there are no problems. No problems with security or what people say or don't say about you, and this is the beauty of life. I don't mind what happens."

I could see why George had become a "non-follower-follower" of Krishnamurti. He was desperately trying to work out the secret. I asked if he had met anyone who understood what Krishnamurti was saying, and who was actually living the teachings. He said he had seen change in others but never felt he had met anyone who had been totally transformed. He waggled his quote fingers around the word "transformed."

"Many, including me, have found an outward freedom, but I've never met anyone who has experienced more than moments of a timeless state. However, I may have met someone and *not* recognized that they were totally free. I mean, what would the criteria be to know if someone was completely free?"

I left George and walked down the street, wondering whether Krishnamurti's message was available only to a few gifted people. The answer came when I found a quote from Krishnamurti at the library: "No matter where you find yourself, no matter what background you come from, no matter what state of mind you're in, you can still clearly look and see what is actually going on, but the observation has to be choiceless and unconditional."

****

I spent the rest of the day walking in the Oak Grove, pondering and formulating my question for Krishnamurti. I wondered if I would have to return to Krishnamurti's talks for the next several decades to understand what he was saying. It was all so new to me, and I found it difficult to identify any burning questions. I wanted to tell Krishnamurti about the experience I'd had at the nightclub and ask him what it meant, but he probably wouldn't consider it a serious-enough question.

Even though Krishnamurti stated clearly that there was no path to freedom, I was convinced that there must be some kind of path, however subtle. I wanted some sort of direction from him, but to where I did not know. I didn't want to *learn* about unconditional freedom—I wanted to *be* unconditionally free. That was my question: How could I be unconditionally free?

chapter four

Duet of One

The Ojai Valley runs along an east-west mountain range, twenty miles inland from the Pacific coastline. The area where Krishnamurti was staying was located at the east-end of the valley surrounded by lush green mountains, oak and pine forests, and acres of orange and avocado groves. The locals call Ojai "Shangri-la," and I could see why. It was the most beautiful place I had ever been.

I arrived early—two hours early—and entered a large, well-kept garden behind an old nineteenth-century redwood house. The lovely property, named Arya Vihara or Noble Abode, was Krishnamurti's former home and where our meeting would take place. He had lived in this house for a number of years but now, during his visits to Ojai, stayed in Pine Cottage, which was behind Arya Vihara. An inviting bench at the far end of the garden was perfectly placed in the shade. It had a good view of the property and the sun-dappled lawns surrounding it. As I sat down, I wondered whether Krishnamurti and other eminent scientists, philosophers, psychologists, and scholars had sat here. I read somewhere that Aldous Huxley had been to Arya Vihara. Huxley, who had been a good friend of Krishnamurti's, claimed that listening to him speak was "[l]ike listening to a discourse of the Buddha—such authority, such intrinsic power." David Bohm, the theoretical quantum physicist, was another regular visitor. Bohm's wife discovered Krishnamurti when she found his book *First and Last Freedom* at the library. She told her husband that Krishnamurti appeared to be speaking about the same wholeness and implicate order[6] that he himself was exploring, although Krishnamurti wasn't using science to describe it. David Bohm found the book "extremely interesting." "What particularly aroused my interest was Krishnamurti's deep insight into the question of the observer and the observed," he wrote. When Bohm contacted him, Krishnamurti reportedly said, "Sir, I've been speaking about this for years and no one is listening." That was the beginning of a thirty year friendship between Bohm and Krishnamurti. Bohm was able to legitimize Krishnamurti within the scientific world and beyond. He made the teachings accessible to those who would normally have shied away from

---

6   *Wholeness and the Implicate Order*, David Bohm, 1980.

what was seen as esoteric Indian mumbo jumbo. I wondered if any of the great thinkers who had visited this property understood what Krishnamurti was talking about and whether they had found unconditional freedom. If they hadn't, what chance did I have? The discouraging thoughts brought on more nerves and forced me from the bench. I saw an opening in the trees and walked along the small path that led into an orange grove. The butterflies in my stomach would have felt right at home here. I could see why Krishnamurti picked this time of year to live in Ojai. The late afternoon light was glorious and the air was filled with the perfume of orange blossoms.

To my delight, the path eventually led to a large, white house, which I instantly recognized as Pine Cottage. I had seen a photograph of the cottage in one of my books. There didn't seem to be anyone around so I walked toward the building. I knew what I was looking for, and there it was: the 100-year-old pepper tree that Krishnamurti had sat beneath as a young man, when he underwent what became known as "the process." He had been unwell for several days, experiencing fever and severe pain in his head and neck. On the third day it was suggested that he rest in the shade of the young pepper tree in the garden, which he did. As the pain eased, Krishnamurti became acutely sensitive and, a few days later, wrote that he had an extraordinary experience while under the tree. "I was in everything, or rather everything was in me." He went on to say, "Like the lake, I felt my physical body, with its mind and emotions, could be ruffled on the surface, but nay, nothing, could disturb the calmness of my soul."[7] I went over to the tree and perched on the stonewall surrounding it. Krishnamurti reported that he could feel the vibrations of Lord Buddha under this very tree. All I could feel was my nervous stomach and the fear of being discovered on private property.

With fifteen minutes to go before the meeting, I made my way back to Arya Vihara and let myself in through the back door. The house was like a chapel, completely quiet. I sat on one of the wooden chairs near the door and listened to the loud tick- tock of the clock counting down the minutes. Something metallic dropped on a hard surface, breaking the silence. It sounded as if it came from the kitchen area. It was 4:57 p.m. and suddenly I questioned whether I was in the right place; I questioned the question I'd memorized; and I questioned why the hell I'd come thousands of miles from home to see an Indian guru who claims not to be a guru, who speaks out against following gurus.

At precisely one minute to five, a cheerful young man appeared and introduced himself as Michael. Later I discovered that Michael was Krishnamurti's personal cook. I followed him down a short corridor to a small conservatory. I could see Krishnamurti through the glass doors. Dressed in grey slacks and a blue shirt, he stood to greet me. Michael opened the

---

7   From Krishnamurti: The Years of Awakening, Mary Lutyens.

door and ushered me in. Two chairs faced each other with a table between them. Both chairs had a view of the garden. Krishnamurti was very welcoming and I thanked him for agreeing to meet with me. We each took a seat and looked out at the garden. The temptation to speak was strong, but I resisted and found the silence to be calming. In those few moments, my nervousness lifted and a deep sense of peace enfolded me. To my surprise, I found myself completely at home in his presence. I could have sat with him and looked out of the window for the whole meeting.

"What would you like to discuss today, sir?"

His words were gentle and I felt no pressure to respond. My question about unconditional freedom was gone. Nothing came—no embarrassment nor panic. I didn't have a care in the world. There wasn't a world. There was only the room and a very serene elderly Indian gentleman sitting opposite. It was a natural feeling of peace. After a few moments, I surprised myself by starting to recount my experience at the nightclub in London and how I had been unable to let it go. I told him I wanted to understand what had happened and why. He listened closely. Mid-story, he leaned across the table and put a hand firmly over my clasped fingers, imploring me to stop.

"Sir, don't get caught up in experiences, no matter how marvelous they seem. Don't go looking for experiences, which are no more than pleasure seeking and gratification. Experiences are time-bound, sir; what *you* are has nothing to do with time.

Experiences, no matter how profound, will not bring you to truth."

He kept his hand on mine, but released the pressure.

"What is it that you are really seeking, sir?" His voice softened.

I wanted to say *this*, this right here, but I did not respond. I just met his gaze.

"What is it that you want most, sir? What is it each one of us wants in this restless world? Isn't it some kind of peace, some kind of happiness, a refuge? You won't find what you are looking for in experiences, sir."

For all those months, I had given my attention to my experiences. Now he was saying that they were insignificant.

"Are you not searching for something permanent? Some lasting certainty—because, in you, is uncertainty?"

I nodded.

"And what is it that you call permanent? Do you want permanent pleasure, permanent gratification, something you can cling too, a permanent experience of happiness without sadness. Perhaps I'm putting this rather sharply, sir." His grip tightened again. "Isn't this what you want, sir?"

Our meeting lasted only twenty minutes, and he did not spare the rod. He stopped speaking and looked at me, perhaps to let his words sink in.

"Sir, when you say that you are seeking to understand your experiences, what is it that you mean? Before seeking something permanent, you must deeply understand the one who is seeking. It is *absolutely necessary* to understand the seeker first and foremost."

He paused to emphasize the gravity of his question, not once taking his eyes off me.

"This cannot be stressed enough, sir. It is *essential* to understand the movement of the seeker, before trying to find out about what you are seeking. Is the seeker different from that which he seeks? Is the seeker any different from the object of his search? Is there a seeker at all? You have to investigate all of this, sir. You have to investigate whether the observer is separate from the observed. Are they different in any way? Don't just take another's word for it. You must find out for yourself. If they are not separate, what are the implications of that finding? What you are lies in the answer."

I had read these words in his books, but hearing them face to face held a forceful urgency.

"Sir, if you know how to look, you will see that the 'experiencer' is *never* separate from the experience. To not see this is a life of sorrow."

His hand still rested on mine in the middle of the table and he did not take his eyes off me, even when he stopped speaking. Once again, I did not respond. I could not respond.

"Sir, the *real* has no opposite. You don't have to seek it. The only sure way to postpone the real is to continue to be a seeker of the real—and to invest your happiness in some experience that you once had or want to have in the future. The real is what *is*; it is the truth and that is the great beauty of it. The moment you seek it, the moment you try to grasp it, you begin to struggle, and the one who struggles can never understand the immensity of this."

He stressed the word "immensity," which seemed to have great meaning for him.

"Look at your own life, sir. Look at the way you are living. Is it not always on the border of sorrow? Are you not trying to escape that sorrow?"

Krishnamurti was right. There was a deep sorrow in me, cleverly disguised by a cluttered mind. At the heart of the sorrow was dissatisfaction—an unquenchable longing.

"Are you not always yearning, sir, always becoming? Becoming is time. Becoming is fear, sir. "I am this now. I will be that in the future." If you look, you will feel the pull of becoming. The pull of yearning, the pull of time."

I knew what he meant, but could not feel the pull of time or a trace of yearning or becoming as I sat there.

"Are you not searching to gain a result, an ending, a place you can say "I have arrived?" Sir, truth is not something to be gained. You don't arrive at truth. It is not a result."

He paused and held my gaze.

"Sir, you must put aside all of your ideas about these petty experiences. Experiences won't bring transformation. Experiences are temporary. *What you are* is the real. To find the real, you must put aside all of your theories, ideologies, all your concepts about truth and freedom—and actually inquire whether you can be psychologically free from dependence. See if there is freedom from fear and anxiety and all your problems. Someone telling you there is such a freedom will do you no good. The key to the door is not someplace else, sir."

He gently patted my hand and looked away for the first time during our meeting. He pulled out his pocket watch. "Sir, we must finish our meeting now as there is another waiting."

As we stood, he reached out for my hand again and held it.

"Find out for yourself if there can be complete unconditional psychological freedom from all problems; something not of time. Start by seeing clearly that the observer is not separate from the observed. Seeing this will end the need for a guru or a savior. You have to look where thought cannot go. You have the flame—all else will follow."

I walked out completely charged with energy. No one had ever spoken to the most hidden part of me. I felt immensely free and happier than I had ever felt in my life.

I went back into the garden and sat on the bench. Krishnamurti's words resonated somewhere inside me. I stayed for a while, absorbing all that was said then walked through the orange grove, certain that I was experiencing what he had talked about. Certain that the observer and the observed were not separate. I *was* the natural state of being and it was extraordinary in comparison with the usual clutter of my mind. This had to be a taste of "something not of time."

****

For the next three days I was calm, peaceful, and joyful, connected to everyone and everything. I met George after one of the talks and he asked me about my meeting with Krishnamurti.

"It was brilliant, George. It was the most real and intense meeting I have ever experienced. He was brutally honest and didn't let me away with anything. This is what freedom must feel like."

To George's credit, he didn't immediately point out that I was experiencing the "private meeting high" reported by almost everyone who had a personal session with Krishnamurti.

****

During the fifth morning talk, I noticed the boundless joy fading and found myself struggling to hold onto the experience. Then it was gone and I was back to working out how to bridge the gap between the experiencer and the experience.

****

On the final day of the talks, I told George that I could understand, now, why people wanted to be around Krishnamurti.

"You see, Ray, while you're in his presence, you get a taste of what he is talking about. It's like a spiritual holiday, where everything works perfectly. It doesn't last, so you go back for a top up."

George said he had met many guru-followers who were trapped in the same cycle. "You are in the perfect state when you are together with him. Then it slowly fades once you leave."

I had never imagined myself getting caught up in the guru circus, but I could see how seductive its power could be. This was the reason Krishnamurti gave emphasis to avoid listening to preachers or following gurus. He said; "be a light unto oneself. Find out who the seeker is."

I had identified the solution. The trouble was, each time I sought the seeker, he couldn't be found.

****

I arrived back in London filled with a fearless optimism. The experience with Krishnamurti, although short-lived, had left me feeling freer than I had ever been. With a better understanding of his teachings, I now knew for sure that there was a completely different way of living, and was determined to solve the conundrum of 'the observer is the observed.'

****

The beauty of Ojai had such a strong impact on me that I wanted Dianne to see the area. She was excited about the idea and we started planning a trip. My suggestion was to spend three weeks away. Dianne had a much better plan.

"Let's take a year off and explore Canada and the U.S.A."

Once we decided to go, everything quickly fell into place. We resigned from our jobs; I sold my flat in London, my car, and everything else I had accumulated over the years. Dianne did the same and we pooled our resources. Once the flat in Reigate was sublet, we organized visas and bought a couple of one-way tickets to New York on Freddie Laker's "no frills" Skytrain.

Within a week of landing in New York we found a used Volkswagen campervan in the small town of Amityville, on Long Island. The van was perfect for us, and we spent the next twelve months living in it travelling through North America, Mexico, and Central America. As promised, I took Dianne to Ojai and showed her the Oak Grove. Unfortunately, Krishnamurti wasn't there at the time, but we were able to attend a few "K" meetings with some of his old students. The group was certainly more experienced with Krishnamurti's teaching than I was, but the meetings, although interesting, weren't helpful at all.

It was a spectacular trip and, after we returned to England, we realized how much our lives and attitudes had changed during that year of "freedom." We loved the adventure of our nomadic life and wanted to see more of the world. Life was full of magical moments and the sense of optimism and fearlessness only grew stronger. There was no way I could go back to my old pointless existence. The quest for a deeper meaning remained a compelling force. My conversation with Krishnamurti remained at the forefront of my contemplations, along with countless liberating talks we had with people on our travels.

Dianne and I never once considered that this way of living might be unsustainable. For the next few years we managed to work and save, and we travelled as much as possible, staying for extended periods in China, India, Nepal, and Southeast Asia.

We had passed through Japan on one of our earlier trips, and eventually ended up living in Tokyo for several years. Dianne mostly taught English and I studied shakuhachi flute as a full-time student and taught English part-time.

After Japan, we returned to England and, within a year, emigrated to Canada, moving to Victoria on Vancouver Island. Once settled, we found jobs there that allowed us to continue spending five or six months of the year overseas.

In 1998, with Dianne's help, I started writing a book about our time in Japan and my studies there. This was published in 2000 along with a CD that I recorded to accompany its release.[8]

Dianne and I were captivated by India from our first visit. The color, the energy, and the people made it into a regular

---

8   Blowing Zen, Finding an Authentic Life - H.J.Kramer /New World Library U.S.A. 2000. New extended Edition 2011. Sentient Publications. C.D Hollow Bell - New Albion Records, U.S.A.

destination for us. We adored the mountains and the scenery of Northern India and preferred to spend our time based in quiet forested areas within touching distance of the snow-covered Himalayan peaks. We set ourselves up in Dharamsala, but after a few years, once it became busy with visitors, moved on to the beautiful ridge high above the mountain town of Almora. When we weren't spending our days trekking in the surrounding mountains, Dianne gave free yoga classes to travelers who were passing through and volunteered at one of the local orphanages. I read books on Indian philosophy and practiced shakuhachi, readying myself for small concerts in Japan.

During one of our winters in Almora, a neighbor who had seen Dianne practicing yoga, suggested that we make a trip to the 'yoga capital' of India in Rishikesh. We rejected the idea, having heard that the town was very busy and a bit of a spiritual circus. A few months later, back in Victoria, an Iyengar yoga instructor of Dianne's mentioned Rishikesh again. He had spent some time there studying with an excellent teacher and insisted that we would love the place. He was right. Rishikesh became our new winter base in India.

Panwali Dwaar, Nanda Devi, Nanda Devi
East Face, Almora, Uttarakhand

chapter five

Mother Ganga

"Hey! Helicopter pilot! Helicopter baba!"

I turned around recognizing my nickname and expected to see Prem baba sitting in his favorite spot on the ghats. Then I remembered: he was gone.

"Helicopter baba. Here. You come . . . one minute only." It was Prem's friend. He gestured frantically with his hand for me to come over. I had a fair idea why the baba wanted to speak to me. I made my way up the steps and sat down next to him.

"You are knowing about my good friend Prem baba?" he said in his heavily accented Indian English.

"Yes," I said, shaking my head in disbelief and commiseration.

"Mother Ganga is taking him. I am only alone now. He is my good friend, you see. I am missing him too much."

"Chai?" I said.

He nodded and accepted my offer.

I had grown fond of Prem over the years. He camped out on the Omkarananda ghats next to the Lakshmi temple and most days we shared the early morning rays of sun that hit that area first. Although his English was quite good, we hardly spoke to each other. If Prem did say something, it was usually about his beloved deity, Lord Shiva. He once tried to explain that Shiva dances the world into existence and plays all parts in this great show of life. For Prem, Shiva was a metaphor for undivided consciousness, the embodiment of all that is. Prem, who never raised his voice in anger, believed that liberation and oneness came through the purifying effects of hashish and meditation. He would spend most of his day completely intoxicated, lying in *savasana*, corpse pose. When I first met him, he had called me helicopter pilot and would use the name whenever he saw me. He had a deluded notion that I owned fifteen helicopters. As odd as that was, the most intriguing part of his delusion was that I had sold one of them. There was no point in asking why I had sold one.

Prem was striking in appearance, with thick dreadlocks coiled high up on his head and many strings of large *Rudraksha seed* prayer beads around his neck. He moved around very little during his day, yet his skinny body was strong and supple. Apart from hashish, he needed almost nothing from the material world except for a few rupees for chai, and his food, which was free from any of the local ashrams.

By nine a.m. Prem would stoke his *chillum* pipe with hashish, set it alight, and shout "Bom Shankar!" across the river, then inhale a lungful of mind-expanding fumes. Enshrouded in a cloud of smoke, Prem played the part of an incomprehensible sadhu, while I played my part as the owner of fourteen helicopters. Prem never asked for money and only once offered me his chillum.

"*Charas*?" I refused and he never offered again.

Prem's death was a tragic accident, but a common one along this holy river. During the monsoons the Ganga in this area swells, becoming a fierce and often destructive force smashing through the community. One morning, while Prem was taking his daily bath, he had unraveled his mass of dreadlocks and bent over into the fast flowing water to wash them. In that moment he was swept away. According to witnesses, as soon as he had dunked his head in the river he was taken with such force that he never stood a chance. Prem's body was never found. Only his soap, shortwave radio, and chillum were left on the step.

We drank our chai and, before I left, I gave Prem's friend a few rupees for tobacco. I continued on my way along the ghats and stopped at the spot where Prem had always bathed and sat for a while. I could picture him scrubbing every inch of his lean, suntanned body in his sacred river. I had a fair idea where Prem's remains would have ended up. There was a dam about four miles away, where the river is diverted to an electric power plant. He would be there, unidentifiable after the pounding his body would have taken from the rocks. Prem would not be alone. I was told that the police regularly pulled out sadhus, pilgrims, and tourists—many because of accidents while bathing, others due to suicide or even murder.

I walked back along the ghats, made my way over to the fruit seller, and bought an orange. As I passed the chai stall, "God" was standing there, hand outstretched.

"Five rupees for one chai only, *saab*?"

That was more like it. Financial sanity had been restored.

****

I was early for my meeting with Rudra. He wouldn't be here for another forty minutes. I made myself comfortable on the step and did a few breathing exercises. Inhaling swiftly, I held my breath for ten seconds and then released it slowly, as if blowing a note down my shakuhachi. I repeated this ten times and then stood and stretched out my back and knees.

The drone from the pious chanting across the river was revitalized by the sounds of laughing children. It was the Monkey Punky Gang, heading my way. I kept my head down hoping to go unseen. No such luck. Pandemonium broke out at the sight of Sachin. They jumped all over me, roughed me up a bit, and made a racket that would disturb the most stoic meditator in Bodh Gaya. It ended when there was no more fun to be had and they scurried off in the direction of the ferry. A few of the children did go to school sometimes. One morning, Dianne and I were on our way to Dayananda Ashram when we walked past an open-air classroom of seven year olds. They were all dressed in maroon sweaters and trousers and sat on the ground in tight rows with their legs crossed. Each child held open an exercise book and looked blank. The teacher was enthroned on a wooden chair in front of them conducting the lesson. We looked away so not to distract them. Then, unexpectedly, from a tiny squeaky voice, coming from the middle of the group, we heard "Monkeee Punkeee!" We scanned the faces and there he was, one of the gang, smiling from ear to ear, not worried about getting a scolding from the teacher.

Talk Two

Rudra settled himself down on the step and commented on the beauty of the morning. He was in the same bright mood as when we last met.

I could feel the warmth of the sun on my face as it slowly made its way over the mountaintops. We sat quietly and, without feeling pressured to fill the silence, waited in a flood of golden light.

"Ray, before we begin this morning, I'd like to make a few suggestions if you don't mind. I can see your commitment and passion, and it seems that you're looking for more than just knowledge of your true nature. Am I correct in assuming this?"

"Yes. There really isn't anything more important to me."

"Then, I must ask you, for the purpose of our talk, to forget everything you know. Forget about your ideas of spiritual awakening or enlightenment and what this or that teacher has said. Do you think you can do that? If you can, then there is the possibility of recognizing a peace and freedom that is limitless and doesn't require any change in normal, everyday life. What do you say?"

"Yes, I can do that. I've been caught in the intellectual understanding for so long, but since our last talk I realize that what I know is useless."

"Yes. You've had some potent experiences that have apparently changed your life in positive ways but, regardless of this, regardless of how grand or transcendental these experiences were, they have always ended, leaving you fragmented and still searching for the *idea* of some kind of wholeness."

"Unfortunately all true. All my efforts have been unsuccessful."

"Okay then. This is an excellent place to begin. No effort is necessary, Ray, no new knowledge required or acquired. No transcendental experience or higher consciousness needs to be achieved. When the recognition of what you are is seen—nothing at all happens. Why would it? You simply find yourself as you already are. Let me give you an example. When you see clearly that an oasis in the desert is a mirage, the appearance of the mirage doesn't go away, but now you are certain that it is not an oasis. It takes a little adjustment to get used to the new perception, but once you see a mirage for what it is, you cannot be fooled into seeing it as an oasis again. The idea of a separate self is no different. Ray, please look and listen with openness and innocence to see what is *actually true.* This may be difficult to do at first but I can assure you, *all* your concepts, theories, and beliefs will be challenged. Are you fine with this?"

"I am."

"If we are to go into this together, it is essential that you are skeptical and doubt everything I say, and I do mean everything. If what I say cannot be confirmed in *actual* experience, then it is a belief. What I am pointing to must be self-evident and beyond doubt. Do you know what I mean by actual experience?"

"Yes. What is happening right now."

"Yes. The direct and immediate experience of sights, images, sounds, tastes, sensation, thoughts. Rather than a story about them. So, can we agree from the onset not to move out of our actual experience into belief?

"Agreed."

"The belief and identification in a *person*, acting in the world, is deeply rooted in us. Since all those around us believe themselves to be personal entities, it's natural to not question this. We are going to scrutinize and dispute this very belief to see that it is the origin of all our misery and unhappiness. You cannot take my word on this. You have to *look* for yourself. This will be demanding."

"I'm fine with that. I want to be completely open and honest with my answers."

"Good. Then together we can explore and discover that the indivisible, timeless nature of awareness does not share the same destiny and limits as the body and thoughts. We are going to look in one place and one place only—this experience, this very aware-presence. You may find yourself wandering off like the prodigal son and getting lost, but I will keep bringing you back home to the certainty and obviousness of this timeless presence. Of course, in reality, you couldn't even take one step away from yourself, never mind get lost. Nor could I possibly bring you back to a home you have never left."

Rudra's words were crystal-clear and delivered with potency and authenticity. As I listened, I intuitively felt I could trust him.

"Ray, when I ask you to look and confirm whether what I've said is true, please don't answer until you can verify it as a fact. This is essential. And let's not be concerned about speaking with any non-dual or spiritually awakened correctness. That can be tiresome. We have to accept the limitations of language when attempting to convey what is most familiar to us, yet beyond words. Words can only point to this formless beauty, this brilliance."

"I can see where language could be limited, Rudra."

"Yes, words are inadequate, but they can also be powerful and expose widely held beliefs. So allow for poetic license and give what we are saying some room to breathe. There will be quite a bit of repetition. Like great music, truth deserves repetition. Don't be concerned if you don't understand something. I will reiterate as many times and in as many ways as possible—until it becomes irrefutable that you are already what you are seeking."

"Yes, please do."

"What we will be inquiring into isn't a new dogma or a religion, nor is it the belief that there is only one mind, or that there are billions of minds out there. This is not about surrendering to a guru or a higher power; this is not about practicing mindfulness, experiencing higher consciousness, or having heightened experiences. Nor is it about believing in *karma* or reincarnation, past lives, or a God in heaven. We are saying something very different here. Questions on such matters are redundant upon realizing that *all* appears, *as you.* Until you see the truth of this, you are seemingly living life through beliefs and theories. Instead we are pointing to the simple, clear truth that there are *not* two things,[9] *you* and *other.* When we use the word *truth,* it refers to absolute truth and not relative truth, which is a belief. And we will have a *mantra*: no matter what you hear, it is much simpler than that. Are you comfortable with the ground rules, Ray?"

Rudra's eyes were bright and his smile was reassuring. I was totally present and felt as if I were standing on the edge of a precipice readying myself to be hurled into space. Then Rudra pounced.

"Do you exist?"

---

9   "Non-duality," from the Sanskrit word Advaita.

"Do I exist? Yes, of course I exist."

"Could I persuade you that you do not exist?"

"No, you couldn't. I exist and I know that I exist."

"Yes, the statement, 'I do not exist,' would be absurd, wouldn't it? To doubt existence, the doubter must be present. Before we know anything else, we must know our own being. 'I am' is the first thing that is known before thoughts and sensations. There is no searching for it or resistance to the knowing of it. It is not just the knowledge that you are. It is the absolute certainty that you are, beyond words. Awareness of this simple 'I am' is happiness itself and, as we said, everyone recognizes happiness. To be happy we do not have to know that it emanates from our own being. We are not concerned with the origin of happiness but, during these moments, we are happy and free. Would this describe those magic moments of yours, Ray?"

"Yes. Happy and free, never questioning why."

"Ray, please tell me about this 'I am.' By what means do you know that 'you are'? What gives you the certainty that you exist? Answer from direct experience."

"Mmm. By what means. . . ?"

"This is not a trick question. You don't have to formulate a response. Who or what is it that knows that you are?"

"I just know that I am. It's obvious. I don't have to believe that I am, or even think about it. *I am*."

"So, you're here, before thought informs you that you're here. You don't have to keep checking, do you?"

"No, of course not. There's no need to check or think about it."

"That's right, but I would like you to look and check anyway. Close your eyes. Do you have to search for yourself to believe that you are? Are you certain that there is no ultimate God, higher self, or imaginary person assuring you that you are?"

"I'm sure. I don't have to believe that I am."

"Yes, that *you are* is undeniable and, does not need any evidence. When I ask you 'by what means do you know that you are,' the answer refers directly to the obvious. Is there anything more obvious than the sense that you are?"

"Not since you pointed it out there isn't."

"Could you describe this sense that 'you are'? Close your eyes again, Ray."

"I don't have any words to describe it. I'm just here. It's just being."

"Yes. Indescribable, beyond description. You understand that I am not using indescribable in any New Age way. What we are going to explore together is not esoteric. What I say can sound esoteric if you miss the simplicity of it. So, lets look again. This time, tell me if you find two things. See if the knowing and the known are separate.

"Do you mean see if there is a knower that knows something?"

"Yes. See if there is *someone* looking at *something* or if there is just one whole experience. Best to close your eyes again."

"Well, there is a sense that *I* am looking at *my* experience; something must know something else."

"Yet, by your own admission, you said that only being could be found. The belief that experience is experienced by 'someone' is the crux of all problems. This sense of separation is the very formation of a personal entity, the illusion of an individual self with a story. From this personal entity, every-thing—body, thoughts, emotions, images—appear separate, creating a personal world of desires, fears, motives, causes, effects, and those wonderfully seductive experiences. Yet, if you look, you will see that your actual experience is indivisibly and inexpressibly *one*."

"What's wrong with stories? I love listening to and telling stories."

"There's nothing wrong with stories. I enjoy a good story too. It's believing that they're real that causes misery. An actor playing Hamlet can become caught in his own performance but when the curtain drops he knows it was a play. All his trails and tribulations were never real. There's no problem playing Hamlet, you have no choice anyway. Believing you are Hamlet, now that's another thing. Okay. We are going to look to see if there is any evidence of two things—an experiencer having an experience. We are going to see whether this is true in actuality.

We are going to look and try and find if there is any direct evidence that you are separate from all that is."

"Saying that there *isn't* an experiencer, someone having an experience, is quite a statement, Rudra. Our life as we know it is based on a subject knowing objects. How would life look if there wasn't an experiencer?"

"It would look exactly like this. As it is, and not how we think it should be or could be. But telling you this has no meaning. You must see it for yourself."

Rudra paused for a moment.

"Okay, Ray, let us look and see if there is any separation between the experiencer and experience? Just relax into ordinary looking. Just as you would look at a bird on a branch if you didn't know its variety. Is there any distance between knowing and that which is known? Please look."

I re-cross my ankles, close my eyes, and try to look deep within.

"There's a mass of sensations, Rudra. The fact that I'm looking at my experience proves that there *are* two things. Someone, me, is looking at something other, my inner experience. There are two things, subject and object. Someone is doing the looking? I'm doing the looking."

"No one is doing the looking. There is the appearance of a sensation with thoughts attached to it. We call this sensation a person. Does a sensation know anything? Does the sensation of sitting on this step, know anything? Or is it just an appearance?

Look closely and you will see that your experience is one seamless whole and not a subject looking at an object. Close your eyes and look again at your experience. Sense deeply that *you* are this indivisible experience."

I stared into the darkness until Rudra's voice broke my concentration.

"Can you find anything but yourself? Or, is there one thing knowing another thing? If there are two things, please point out where the boundary is? Where you end and experience begins."

"I know that 'I am' without referring to anything but, when I look, there are lots of sensations and thoughts whizzing about. There are many experiences going on at once, Rudra."

"So says thought. But is it true? Can you have more than one experience at a time?"

Rudra went quiet.

"Okay, let's try this. Place your hands on the step, either side of you, and close your eyes."

I did as he asked and waited for his next instruction. Somewhere behind me, I could hear a group of donkeys trotting by. The bell on the lead donkey tinkled and the donkey *wallah* scolded them. The Parmarth Ashram clock chimed once. It must be 9:30 a.m.

"Look carefully. How many experiences are there?"

I wanted to say many, then four, then two. As I relaxed, I saw it!

"There is only one experience."

"Is there one 'thing' knowing another 'thing'?"

"No. There's just experience."

"Okay. Now, how near or how far is the experience of what we call this 'step' from the sense that you are?"

I could see what he is getting at and answered quickly.

"No distance. There is no distance at all, but I want to say..."

"Wait. Not so fast. Look again. I want you to make sure that there are not two experiences. Can you find any boundary between the sensation of the step and this obvious sense that 'you are'?"

"I keep feeling that it is *me* touching the step. Me having an experience."

"Thought is saying you're touching the step. But can you find a boundary?"

"No. There's just the experience. I see what you're saying."

"Yes, Ray. One seamless experience. You cannot find a subject-object relationship. It is just as it is. There's not something sensing something else."

"Yes. I see that. Amazing!"

"Ray, you cannot experience two things because there are not two things, *ever*. Only thought could say that there are two or more experiences. And thought is not what you are."

"Yes, but we need thought, Rudra. It's essential in daily life."

"We are not trying to do away with thought and all its apparent usefulness here. Thought is not the enemy. We are not trying to control thought. Thought is not a problem. Ownership of thought is. The belief in a 'thinker' is."

He placed his hand on my shoulder

"Ray, tears will not stop flowing nor laughter appearing with the discovery of what you truly are. You're not going to float off on a cloud of bliss and live on light. It's not the end of what is apparently essential. This is not the end of emotions and compassion. On the contrary, without the illusion of a suffering personal entity, with all of its 'thought stories,' there is no one to judge or reject anything. Even the concept of acceptance and letting go is not there. Who would let go or accept what? There would have to be a controller to be able to accept or let go. Without the illusion of a personal entity, there is no one who could possibly want the situation to be different."

"Many seekers hear this and say, well, if there's no controller, I can do anything I like. If nothing matters, why do anything?"

"Thought says all kinds of things, Ray."

"You never accept or reject or judge, Rudra? You never get angry?"

"Anything can show up but there is no ownership. Nothing is denied. Rejecting and judging appear. But nothing is believed to be true. Just like our friend Hamlet on the stage; your part is played but you're not caught up in your own performance. So, Ray, you looked and found *something* that cannot be put into words, an actual experience that is not a belief or a story. You cannot find two things. Only thought says there is more than one and that something is looking at something else. Don't move on until you are sure you have seen this clearly."

"Yes, unless I think about it, there is only experience."

Rudra tilted his head and sniffed the air.

"Ray, can you find any separation between the smell of the air and the awareness of it?"

I breathed in deeply. There was a faint smell of smoke from the funeral pyres burning in the distance.

"... There's no separation between the smell and the awareness of it. I'm getting this. There's only smelling."

"Yes Ray, just smelling."

He reached into his pocket, pulled out a tube of mints, unwrapped them, and offered me one.

I thanked him and placed the mint in my mouth.

"Ray, how far is the taste from the knowing of it?"

"No distance. There is just experience."

"Yes Ray, unadorned experience. Awareness and the taste are not in any way separate, are they? Now I am going to ask you to look at *all* that is showing up as experience: body, taste, touch, smell, feelings, emotions. How near or how far is the experience of *all* that shows up from the knowing of it?"

I closed my eyes, touched the step on either side of me, listened to the sounds, smelled the air, tasted the mint. As I looked, thoughts and sensations began to calm into one direct experience. Thought kept butting in with descriptions and stories—but there was only one experience. Indivisible, beyond description. Excited, I blurt out my discovery.

"Rudra, all there is, is experience!"

"Not even that, Ray. *That* which remains, when all distinctions and reactions are no more, is indescribable."

"This is extraordinary, Rudra."

Rudra laid his hand on my arm, as if to stop me moving into the story of what I had found. We remained in silence for a few minutes.

"This is a good place for us to stop today, Ray. If you have time, please stay for a while and go through all that we have looked at this morning. See if you can find any error in what you have seen. Ray, the imagined separate self cannot stand the dispassionate light of enquiry. The separate self is as real as a mirage in the desert. Keep looking at experience and test it out."

chapter six

Neat and Clean

Usha Devi, the Swiss-born Maharani of Omkarananda Ganga Sadan, which is a small ashram guesthouse on the river, was holding an early morning staff meeting and thundering out her disappointment at yesterday's forgotten instructions. The ashram staff looked on, confused, probably wondering why they must clean the tops of doors, *under* the fridge, picture frames, surfaces of fans—every day, even if they're still clean from yesterday? And why must the toilets be cleaned constantly?

I was sitting at the entrance waiting for Rudra to arrive. Usha glanced at me. "My God. What to do? It's terrible, really. Every day I have to say the same things over and over again."

Usha turned her attention to Binod, the front desk manager. He was sitting in his usual spot on a swivel chair. Posted on the wall above him was a list of rules for the ashram—no meat, no alcohol, no drugs, no smoking, no shoes, no music, no noise. Usha was shouting at him in Hindi and Binod was giving as good as he was getting. Binod could ruin any illusions yoga students might have about their spiritual advancement, their "peace of mind," their "shanti." Polite and pleasant greetings, courteous inquiries, and civil requests were of no interest to him. Western swamis, dreadlocked hippies, Brazilian saints, serious yogis, senior yoga teachers—he has seen them all come through the glass doors of Omkarananda guesthouse, and he was never impressed. He would *always* out-shout the best of them. With the decibel level of a street hawker, Binod could shatter the deepest *savasana* in a second.

Once satisfied that everything was under control, Usha disappeared into the yoga hall to do her own practice.

I've stayed in countless different places in India and know that this ashram is truly a rare spot, thanks to Usha's Germanic precision and tireless efforts. She had travelled the world by the time she arrived here in the early eighties, and she has lived here ever since. In those days, she says, elephants still crossed the river and there was only one bridge down in Lakshman Jhula. Longing for some structure and peace, she eventually met Swami Omkarananda and joined the Omkarananda

Ashram, but never wanted to take the robes of a *sannyāsin*.[10] She wanted to dedicate herself to the service of others through her work at the ashram, but also wanted to become a wife and mother. Her husband, Prabhuji, and their son, Siddhartha Krishna, who was brought up in the tradition of yoga, are both brilliant scholars and teachers of Vedanta.

Omkarananda Ganga Sadan,(Guest House) Lakshmi Temple and ghats. Photo: Sebastian Caussade

Usha is extraordinary and, as a woman living and working in a male-dominated country, she has to have a tough exterior, which any guest can crack through if they stay long enough. She simply cannot hide the light that shines.

---

10 Renunciate initiated into "Truth" by a master.

She did not formally add the study of asana yoga postures to her philosophical studies until the early nineties, when she found her guru, B.K.S. Iyengar. His precision matched her predilection for order. She found the piece that had been missing in her searching. She started running the guesthouse, and the small yoga hall was eventually enlarged into Patanjala Yoga Kendra. After a number of years of devoted study and practice, Guruji announced that it was time for her to begin teaching yoga asana in Rishikesh.

When Usha is not teaching yoga to overflowing classes of students from all over the globe, she runs a successful prep school that she started for the ashram. She is also involved in supporting some very remote schools in the hills of Uttarakhand. Several years back, Usha heard that there was a group of children living in the Haridwar prison with their mothers. In India, mothers and pregnant prisoners that are locked up for life are allowed to keep their young children with them if their family won't take the responsibility. The children can stay with their mothers until they are seven years old and then they are sent to an orphanage. The children at the jail receive no proper education during their time there, and have nowhere to play. Usha rallied her students and friends and funded the creation of a prison preschool, which she equipped with toys, books, and a play area with swings. Moreover, she persuaded the head of the prison to let a driver take the children to a nearby public school every day.

Last week, Dianne helped Usha to deliver much-needed things for the women and children. The yoga students had collected packets of biscuits, soap, incense, coloring books, toys, and warm clothes. Dianne said when they arrived, the kids came racing over to cuddle Usha, and they touched her feet as a sign of respect.

****

Rudra arrived on time, eager to meet Dianne before our meeting. I asked him to sit and wait while I went to get her.

I peeked through the door of the yoga hall and witnessed a scene of terrible cruelty, with aspirants hanging upside down, tied-up, or strapped in strange positions with huge weights pinning their legs to the ground. Usha was standing on the sidelines, relaying some hilarious experience to Dianne. When I eventually waved Dianne over, she quickly wrapped a sarong around her waist and joined us in the reception area. Rudra greeted Dianne with namaste. Without hesitation she returned the gesture.

In the two of them, I saw light meeting light; I was delighted that they had finally met. We sat in white plastic chairs and I listened as they chatted. Rudra told Dianne that he, too, practiced yoga and does a morning routine before his daily walks along the ghats. He talked about how his daughter, in Singapore, nagged him to do a few poses every day and take care of himself. He also mentioned that he has a son in New

York and that his wife passed away four years ago. He talked about his family home in Sister's Bazaar and told her that we are welcome to use it any time, if we can cope with the cold. The meeting was interrupted when Binod stormed across the reception area and bellowed up the stairwell to the cleaning ladies on the third floor.

Dianne invited Rudra to join us for lunch one day, and then we left for our morning talk on the ghats.

We arrived at our spot just as the coffee wallah was passing with what looks like a large metal bucket containing an aluminum kettle. Tied to the handle of the bucket are several long tubes of tiny, stacked plastic cups and the ubiquitous dirty old rag.

"Coffee, Ray?"

"Yes, good idea. Thank you."

The coffee wallah set the container down next to us and, as he lifted the heavy kettle out of the bucket, I could see below it red-hot pieces of charcoal glowing in a bowl. With experienced hands, he removed the tiny plug from the spout, put it between his teeth and then, with typical Indian panache, quickly poured scalding coffee into the first cup and handed it to me. I took it gently by the rim, careful not to let the flimsy plastic collapse between my fingers. Rudra paid the man and then we watched as he organized everything back into its place. An emaciated looking sadhu sitting a few yards from us looked over and wobbled his head as only Indians can do. Here, I took it to mean, "If there's an extra coffee going around, I'll take it." I handed the coffee wallah another three rupees and told him to take a cup to the sadhu.

Dianne, co-writer, in the Yoga Hall - Patanjala Yoga Kendra, Omkarananda Ganga Sadan, Rishikesh

Rudra held his tiny cup up to me. "Just what the doctor ordered. Nothing like a good cup of coffee—and this is nothing like a good cup of coffee. Thankfully, one of the better things your British relatives left behind was tea."

"Hey, don't forget jelly and custard. We left that, too. Oh, and of course cricket."

"Cricket is an English game?"

"Very funny. We should never have taught you the rules."

The sadhu, enjoying his coffee, gave us a smile and, this time, a thank-you wobble of his head.

"Rudra, before I forget, have you heard of a sadhu who lived in Rishikesh during the late sixties, early seventies. His name was Tat Wale baba."

"Tat Wale baba. Yes, indeed. I'm surprised to hear that name after so many years. How on earth do you know about Tat Wale?"

"I have a friend who is writing a book on some of the lesser-known saints of India and Dianne and I are doing some research for him while we're here."

"He died sometime back in the seventies, I think." He pointed across the river into the hills. "See the area where the trees are taller than all the others? Can you see the tallest tree? It's a huge banyan. That's where Tat Wale's old ashram is. He used to live there all year round. He was a good man."

"Are there people still living up there?"

"That I don't know. I haven't been up there for many, many years."

"Do you think it would be possible to go and see the place?"

"I don't see why not. There's probably still a path, but even if you know roughly where it is, it won't be easy to find your way through the forest. You'll have to ask a local to give you directions. Look for someone older though, someone who might remember the place. Be careful, it's easy to get lost up there. It's a beautiful forest, but elephants roam through the area and I've heard rumors of criminal types, we say *dacoits*, living higher up, hiding from the police. If you do go, use the banyan tree as a marker."

Talk Three

"Before we begin our enquiry this morning, Ray, what is our mantra?"

My vacant look prompts him to tell me the answer.

"No matter what you hear, it's much simpler than that. Okay. Do you have any questions from our last meeting?"

"Yes, I do have a couple, Rudra. I went over everything we've looked at and I can see that touching, tasting, and smelling sensations show up as one complete, indescribable experience. But I'm having difficulty with hearing and seeing. They seem to happen at a distance, so I can't confirm that they are not separate from me. They certainly feel separate."

"Yes, that's why I left them until now."

Rudra stared across the river as though he was trying to pick something out, but then turned and looked upriver toward the smoking funeral pyres.

"Ray, where does the experience of 'you' end and the sound of those barking dogs begin? Is there a boundary or distance between 'you' and the sound of the barking? Not what thought says about sound or distance, just your actual experience. No need to strain to hear; listen in a relaxed manner."

"There is just sound, Rudra. But my thoughts are telling me that the sound is over there, at a distance."

"Stay with your actual experience. Until thought tells you otherwise, you cannot say where 'you' start and where the sound begins, can you?"

"Well, without thinking about it, the sound is not at a distance and I can't find a boundary where I end and the barking begins."

"So, Ray, there is no *hearer* and *heard,* only *hearing,* yes? Look and listen again."

"Yes, there's just hearing."

"If we don't call it 'hearing,' we could say that it is an indivisible experience, which cannot be described."

"Yes, it's just what it is."

"Right. Whatever we choose to call experience, it is only ever the familiarity of our own aware-beingness. Beingness knowing itself."

"Yes, but I have to say, it was easier to grasp with sensations that are closer to my body."

"Ray, hearing is the same as everything else we've observed—experience without a thought story."

"I'm beginning to see that thought is the storyteller in this grand show, Rudra."

"There isn't a storyteller. Thought *is* the story. Thought is claiming, 'I am experiencing this, I am experiencing that,' when there is only experience. Thought cannot know this experience, this aware-beingness. It is like a wave trying to control the vast ocean. And like a wave, which is never separate from the ocean, thought is never separate from awareness. Ocean knows only ocean. Awareness knows only awareness. Thought does not know awareness; thought does not know *you*. It only thinks that it does. Thought says you are this or you are that, but awareness is not affected by whatever shows up. Take a few minutes to see the truth of this, Ray."

I rubbed my temples and probably looked a little dazed.

"Yes, I get what you're saying. Thought doesn't know awareness."

"That's right but, saying that you 'get it' is not enough. You have to see it clearly. The difference between what you actually known and, what you 'think' you know, is huge. Thought is an experience just like any other experience and, experience is not subjective. Once you see that thought is harmless, it can dance all it likes until it tires from lack of attention. Let's continue with our investigation into hearing and seeing, shall we? Look at that ashram across the river."

Rudra pointed toward Ved Niketan, its walls shimmering pink in the sun.

"Is there a seer and a seen of that ashram? Without looking for an answer, where do you, awareness, end and the ashram begin? Point out the boundary if you can find one."

I stared across the river and immediately veered toward a story of how ridiculous it seemed that I was not separate from the ashram.

"I can't find a boundary Rudra, but it seems incomprehensible from what I know about space and distance. I am here. The ashram is way over there."

"Yes, you have the belief that you and the ashram are separate. Look as a baby would look at its mother. Let thought appear with its story, but you tell me your *actual experience*. Now, how far is the ashram from you, from awareness?"

I took a deep breath, exhaled slowly."

"Without thought telling me about it there is no distance between me and the ashram. There is no observer. There's just seeing. That's extraordinary."

"Yes. Not even seeing. Your actual experience is that the seeing and the seen are one. If that is the case, there cannot be any separation, can there? That's Krishnamurti's 'observer *is* the observed right there! Just this, as it is. Only the inexpressible."

"But I got only a glimpse that there is no separation."

"So says thought. Only thought can say that there is separation and that you only had a glimpse. There has never been separation *ever* and nothing needs to change to realize this. This is not a new event. There is only the *belief* that knowing is separate from the known. Actual experience *always* shows you the falseness of this. Please look again and see the truth of this."

I closed my eyes for a moment then opened them: The ashram was not at a distance. There was only experience without resistance—and a sense that there was not even that!

Rudra noticed my excitement and laughed.

"Yes Ray, only *this*. *All* of this present scene has no here or there, no boundaries. All takes place as *you*. *You, awareness,* are simply the knowing of yourself, as *everything*."

"There is no one looking. There's only. . ." Rudra interrupted me before I could finish.

"Yes, Ray. Why bother giving it a name?"

"Truly miraculous."

"Isn't it?"

For the first and only time, I saw Rudra ever so slightly wobble his head. We were quiet as we watched hundreds of cormorants take flight. When they were high enough, they formed a V-shape and headed up river. Without a hint of separation, the scene and I were one. I *was* the scene. I felt light, free, and open. I tried not to bubble over too much with excitement.

Rudra did not allow me to be jubilant for long.

"Now it gets really interesting, Ray. Tell me: Perception, sensation, thought, feeling, and emotion are appearing as you, awareness. Where are you located?"

"Well, I want to say here," I said, tapping the side of my head. "Or here," I patted my chest. "But I know what you're going to say."

"Yes, you do. What we call head or body is only experience and not separate from the knowing of itself. You, awareness, know of them as experience. They do not know of you. So, can you find any location if nothing is separate and *you* are all that is?"

I took a couple of minutes to look around at the scene, as if for the first time.

"I can't, Rudra. Not unless thought says there is a location."

"Can you find anything that is outside of you, awareness?"

"No. Not unless thought says there is."

"Can you find anything that *isn't* you? Can you find anything that is not this indivisible oneness?"

"No . . . How could I have missed this?"

"You, awareness, have never missed this. The simple knowing of our own being is always overlooked because thought says oneness cannot be so. Thought couldn't come close to describing *this*, could it? Thought gives the illusion that it is the controller and can turn oneness into many. But thought is just an appearance, like any other appearance. Where is thought's place in this beauty and love?"

"It's astonishing, Rudra. Until now it seemed that thought was in the foreground and awareness in the background. It's the other way around, isn't it?"

"No, it's not the other way around, it is neither. Be clear on this, Ray. That would be two things. Foreground and background are just thoughts about a foreground and a background."

"What about the unconscious mind?"

"What about it? Look at your actual experience. Nothing is ever hidden. The sense that there is something unconscious is just a thought, a sensation. Mind is just thoughts appearing as awareness. What you are calling the unconscious mind is no other than a theory, a thought story. Thought seeks to change actual experience for something better, creating the illusion of before and after, of time and space. Thoughts of another apparent time and place *always* appear, right here, right now. *You, awareness* are another name for *oneness*. You have never *not* been oneness, and oneness has no dimension or location. It is all there is. Let's be quiet for a while in the obviousness of aware-presence—awareness only knowing awareness."

I closed my eyes and leaned back against the step.

"All we are doing here, Ray, is pointing to the real, which you, awareness, alone are. The real is always real. Gold, no matter what it appears as, is never anything other than gold. Whether the gold 'takes on the appearance' of a ring or a statue those apparent objects only ever appear as gold and only seemingly come into existence."

"What do you mean, the ring and the statue only seemingly come into existence?"

"The ring or statue is only an appearance. Only the gold exists. There is only ever gold. There is only ever *you*."

"Are we using gold as a metaphor for consciousness?"

"Any label is fine if it communicates this inexpressible 'isness.' Awareness is the real. Or, we could say that consciousness is all there is."

"So, everything is unfolding as consciousness?"

"Nothing is unfolding. Time would be required for something to unfold. There is only ever the *one*, appearing as the dream of many. Only a 'personal entity' could believe that something is unfolding, and there isn't one."

We were quiet for a while.

"Ray, we have covered quite a bit of ground this morning. Let's stop now."

"Yes, that sounds good, Rudra."

"I have to go to Mussoorie tomorrow for about week. If you'd like, we can meet again next Thursday after I get back, unless it's raining, of course."

"Yes, Thursday would be great."

"Until then, investigate all that we've examined so far. Look for any errors. See if any separation can be found anywhere."

Rudra pressed his hands onto his knees and stood up.

"Ray, thought knows nothing of the real. Thought doesn't know this peace and cannot touch this love. And where there is love, there is not a hint of fragmentation or fear. *You* alone are the real."

chapter seven

The Game of Death

Dianne and I had been watching the shrouded, triangular shape of a meditator sitting on the ghats day and night for a week. We could see him from our balcony four hundred yards away. For the first five days, we thought nothing of it. After all, he was not an uncommon sight in Rishikesh. When I mentioned him to one of the ashram cooks, she said that she'd seen him there for much longer than seven days.

Concerned about his health, Dianne had decided to keep an eye on him to see if he moved or changed position throughout the day.

I walked past him on several occasions and was impressed at how upright and still he was. Once or twice, I stopped and leaned in close to see if he was breathing. Others slowed down to watch, more curious about my behavior than about the figure on the ground. "Do you think he's okay?" I asked them. Their responses were similar.

"He is doing *sadhana*, sir."

"This is his spiritual practice, sir."

"He is in deep meditation, you see, sir."

"He is in a very deep state of *samadhi*. He should not be disturbed."

On the morning of the eleventh day, the meditator was slumped forward and by the afternoon looked as if he had caved in completely. Was he sleeping or *dead*?

On the twelfth day, he was lying flat on his back, covered from head to toe in his blanket. Now he looked more like a corpse than a meditator. If he was doing a special discipline, why hadn't he chosen a quieter place along the river? It didn't feel right, but I had no idea what to do.

My resolve not to interfere wavered and within an hour I was back with a bottle of water, three bananas, and a packet of biscuits. I touched his shoulder and told him that he should drink and eat something. No response. I left the water and food next to him.

When I arrived the next morning, he was still lying in the corpse position with his bare feet sticking out of the blanket now. I touched his ankles. They were cold and felt lifeless. The water and biscuits were untouched, but two banana skins were lying next to him.

"Hello sir. Are you all right? Do you need help? Can I get you anything?" I asked. Still no response.

On the fourteenth day, I removed the blanket from his face. His eyes were closed and he didn't move. His skin was cold to the touch and his lips cracked and dry.

"Sir, are you all right?"

He was a young man, perhaps in his early thirties. His head was shaven with a shadow of new growth. He was wearing the thin maroon robe of a sannyāsin. It was soaked through and I could smell urine. I touched his neck and felt a pulse. He moved a little.

"What is your name, sir?" There was no answer. I rubbed his head and tried to revive him.

A group of French tourists stopped to look and started taking photographs. Their Indian guide warned me not to get involved in what he considered none of my business and then herded the group to their next spiritual encounter. Perhaps good advice, but I couldn't bring myself to leave.

I stopped a man and asked if he could help me.

"I'm sorry, sir, I cannot help you. It's not like in your country. If we help him, he will be our responsibility. If he dies, sir, we will have to pay the funeral costs. If we call the police, they can make many problems for us, you see. If he lives, we will be liable for his hospital bills. Sir, just leave him in peace. He may want to depart this world. Many are coming from all over India to die here, next to this sacred river. It is most auspicious to go from here."

I asked him if he knew someone I could call, a doctor or a hospital.

"Sir, there are many such cases within walking distance of this very spot. No one will come. He is doing what he wants to do. It is best that you leave him to his own karma."

Maybe, but I felt that I had no choice. According to the same rulebook, maybe it was my karma to help him.

I lifted his head and put the bottle to his mouth, forcing him to drink a little water, only to have him spit it out with a fair bit of force.

"What's your name?"

He opened his eyes and seemed overjoyed to recognize me.

"You are Govinda."

"What is your name, my friend?"

"I am Bruuuce Leeee. Bruuuce Leeee."

"Pardon?"

"I am Bruce Lee. You are Govinda."

"You must drink some water, Bruce Lee."

"No water," he whispered.

"You'll die without water, Bruce Lee. Where are you from?"

He said something that was almost inaudible. I asked him to repeat it and moved my ear closer to his mouth.

"Madhuban."

Madhuban Ashram was in Kailash gate, only a fifteen minutes' walk from where Bruce lay. There's a Hari Krishna temple on the ashram grounds. Bruce was a Hari Krishna devotee.

"I'll get help for you, Bruce Lee."

I pulled my woolen hat onto his head, tucked the blanket around him again, and covered his feet.

"You are Govinda. I am Bruce Lee."

The head swami at the Hari Krishna temple knew Bruce, but called him by his temple name. I could only catch the last part: Ananda. I told him exactly where Bruce was located and stressed the urgency of his condition. He seemed unmoved and slightly annoyed, but said that he would take care of the situation.

I was relieved to have finally found someone who would take responsibility for the young man. Feeling more relaxed, I stopped at the Hari Krishna restaurant on the temple grounds for a *lassi*.

Dianne and I often ate here, so the young waiter knew me and began chatting as I ordered my drink. I told him about Bruce Lee Ananda and my meeting with the swami. When he returned with my lassi, his demeanor had changed and he didn't make eye contact.

"Do you know Bruce Lee?"

He was silent, but wobbled his head indicating that he did.

"What's going on?"

"This is a most difficult situation, you see, sir," he whispered. "They are asking him to leave, you see, sir, for causing the nuisance. He is making many problems and not following ashram rules. He is disturbing others and making noise, sir."

I finished my drink and left the restaurant. Bruce was not my problem anymore.

****

It rained hard overnight and, in the morning, out of habit, Dianne went to the balcony to look.

"Would you believe it? He is still there, Ray. He must be frozen to the bone."

Bruce was still lying horizontal in exactly the same place.

Concerned, I spoke to a few of the workers in our ashram. They all agreed that Bruce should be allowed to follow his own karma. I decided to take their advice and not get involved. Once again, however, my resolve weakened. I needed help. Rudra was still away for two more days and by then I might be paying for the wood for Bruce's funeral.

Then I remembered my friend, the owner of Flavors restaurant in Muni Ki Reti. Rajesh would know what to do.

"There is one place possible," Rajesh said. "One German woman who is running a leper colony up in Tapovan might help you. It is not too far. I'll get a taxi driver to take you there."

The taxi driver dropped me off at the front gate of the Sivananda Home. I told the gatekeeper that there was an urgent matter and that I needed to see the German matron. He asked me to wait and disappeared inside the building. Several minutes later he returned, opened the gate, and let me in. I was escorted to a room with six beds that were all occupied.

"Please sit here." The porter said, pointing to a wooden chair by the door. "Please wait. Madam is busy. She will see you when she is free."

A cleaner with a mop and bucket was slowly swishing around the ward, side to side, corner to corner. The place reeked of disinfectant. A delicate young man, missing part of his nose, came rushing over and sat down at my feet. Each time I looked at him and smiled, he began to cry, so I looked away, allowing him to stare at me. There was a male nurse in the far corner, bathing and dressing a horrific wound on what was left of a man's foot. I remembered Rajesh's parting words.

"You won't be able to eat anything for a while after you leave the colony."

Fifteen minutes had gone by and there was no sign of the German woman. I stood up to stretch my legs. The young man on the floor started to blubber again. I quickly sat back down and looked away. After another ten minutes, I decided to move to a chair I could see in an adjacent room. I got up and headed across the hall at a rapid pace. Crybaby jumped up, followed me just as fast, and ended up back on the floor staring up at me.

There were only two patients in this room, both attempting to watch a cricket match between India and England on a battered television. The picture was rolling and a huge static snowstorm blew across the field.

"What's the score?" I asked a little too loudly. The sound of my voice set Crybaby off and he was in tears again.

I'm sorry," I said, patting his head. "Are you all right?" I asked in Hindi. This seemed to calm him down. He folded his arms placed them on my knees and rested his forehead. He seemed to enjoy having his head patted, so I continued.

"He is *pagal*," said one of the patients, shaking what remained of his right hand by the side of his head. Crazy.

"Oh, you speak English," I said. Which was a stretch, considering that I had only "He is" to go on.

"Leg before wicket, silly mid-on, sticky wicket, howzat, rain stop play. Out!" he shouted.

He pointed to the television indicating I should fix the picture. I got up, which caused Crybaby to break down and sob, and I held the aerial high above my head. The picture stopped rolling. The patient with two good hands applauded. I was imagining myself standing there until the end of the five-day test match when a stout woman entered the ward, shouting commands in Hindi. Crybaby darted out of the room like a frightened bird. I let go of the aerial to moans of disappointment from the two cricket fans. The snow blizzard in Kolkata resumed and was now virtually a whiteout.

She got straight to the point.

"What do you want?"

I could tell immediately by her accent that she was not German, but Dutch.

After I had finished telling her about Bruce's fifteen-day event on the ghats, she looked irritated and tutted loudly.

"Who told you to come here?"

"No one madam. I couldn't think of anywhere else to go. Bruce will die if he doesn't get help quickly."

She shouted out an order in Hindi, which I could just make out. She was sending an ambulance and a driver to pick Bruce up.

"Go with the driver and bring him back here." Frowning, she stormed off down the corridor.

Bruce was cold, wet, and seemingly in critical condition by the time we arrived. The driver brought a blanket and I carried a rolled-up stretcher, which was nothing more than sackcloth affixed to two bamboo poles. We covered Bruce and I began to rub his feet. A man saw what I was doing and stopped, knelt down next to me and started to rub Bruce's thin legs vigorously. Then another man stopped and another and another. Soon there were eight people. The driver said that Bruce had a weak pulse; we must move quickly. We didn't bother with the stretcher and together carried Bruce to the ambulance. "Turn on the siren," I told the driver, "and drive as fast as you can."

With no beds available, the matron had placed a mattress on the floor in the middle of the ward. The porters carried Bruce in and laid him down, covering him with more blankets. One of the male nurses wheeled in an intravenous drip and another brought a syringe. The matron knelt by Bruce's side, placed her hand on his brow, and spoke to him firmly in English.

"What have you been doing to yourself, young man? My God, look at the mess you're in. What is your name?"

Bruce mumbled and started to writhe quite violently. The nurse held him down as the matron expertly found a vein and injected him. Bruce became still. There were more commands and a porter brought a pair of scissors, another carried in a pail of hot water. The matron began cutting off Bruce's robe and then stopped and stared at me.

"Wait outside."

I went into the corridor and sat on a wooden bench. The cricket commentary blared down the corridor and Crybaby was back at my feet. I patted his head.

Twenty minutes later the Dutch matron appeared carrying a writing pad and a pen.

"Please write a letter promising that you will never come back to this hospital again and that you will not mention to anyone that you were here. We cannot handle more patients! This letter will relieve you of any responsibility. You do not want responsibility for this man, I can assure you."

She turned and left the ward.

chapter eight

Bicycle Baba

The holy city of Rishikesh began disturbing its beloved Gods by four a.m. with the reciting of Vedic verses and the chanting of devotional *bhajans*. Dianne and I, lying in bed, but wide awake, listened to the sounds so familiar after many years. We had talked well into the night about my meetings with Rudra and neither of us had slept much.

"Let's go for a walk," Dianne said with a rush of energy.

We dressed quickly, putting on multiple layers against the morning chill. Dianne grabbed an open packet of biscuits from the cupboard and stuffed them into her jacket pocket.

"Why are you taking those?"

"Just in case the dogs get funny."

The dogs are usually friendly during the day, but after dark they roamed in packs and could get territorial or "funny," as Dianne would say.

As quietly as possible, I slid the heavy bolt latch into position and snapped the padlock shut on our door. Downstairs, Kishan, the night watchman, gazed at his phone, the screen lighting up his face. Surprised when he sees us, he asked if everything was okay. With a noisy clatter of keys, he unlocked the front door and released us out into India.

It was still dark, but the ashram lights illuminated the ghats just enough for us to see. Lying against walls, in corners, and on benches, sleeping people resembled corpses, shrouded from head to foot under thick blankets. Some lay curled up with dogs, sharing warmth and fleas.

Below the telephone exchange building, lying in the trapped white sand from last year's floods, three large cows were sleeping. One lay on its side and, having never seen that before, I wondered if it was dead. A few yards away, in a dip in the sand, a pig and her babies were snuggled together. On the periphery of the enclosure, a dog had dug a small bed for himself and was curled up in a tight ball.

We walked close to the water's edge and slowed down to look at the paraphernalia left from one of last night's funerals. A woman's long red *dupatta* scarf lay discarded in a pile and the flagstone step was stained with lamp oil from the smashed clay pots. Scattered around were bits of cut string, used to tie the body to the makeshift bamboo stretcher. Two razor blades lay next to the remains of a husband's or sons' black hair.[11]

We reached the place where I meet Rudra and sat next to the rushing water. There was just enough light in the sky now to silhouette the foothills on the other side of the river. I repeated Rudra's words from one of our talks. "Awareness of this is wonderful but words cannot find the beauty and the love of simply being this."

In the distance, we heard the single strike of the clock tower announcing that it was 5:30 a.m.

"I'm getting cold, Ray. Let's walk back."

On the way, I noticed that the "dead" cow was sitting up.

Back in our neighborhood, the day's activity has begun. Two sannyāsin, both in orange woolen hats and thick orange shawls over their robes, passed us, their flip-flop sandals slapping in a rhythm discordant with the drumming coming from an ashram. A few of the corpses were now sitting up, rubbing their heads, and scratching their skeletal bodies.

Dianne returned to the ashram to get ready for her morning practice and I sat on the step next to the Lakshmi temple. I

---

11 In Hinduism, the male members of the family are expected to shave their heads when a loved one dies. Hair is a symbolic spiritual offering, representing humility and the letting go of ego. It is a sacrifice of beauty, hence shaving your head shows your grief and sincerity for the departed soul.

could hear the tones of a lethargic chant and, close by, someone was ringing a hand bell.

The sound made me smile as I recalled the ice-cold bottles of school milk we drank on frosty mornings during playtime: I've just shot my mate Terry. I'm much faster to the draw than he is. He hits the ground convincingly and I place the gun back in my holster. The school bell rings, but Terry won't get up, can't get up. A circle of excited kids taunt him. Terry's gripping his arm and crying out in pain. He's not mucking about. He's really in trouble. I get the teacher and, within ten minutes, an ambulance whisks Terry away to the hospital. He's broken his arm.

The sadhu from Brahmananda Ashram limped down the steps. One of his legs is shorter than the other. He was carrying three small steel containers and using a long bamboo pole for support. Without fail, he arrived at six a.m. to bathe in the river and offer his gratitude and prayers to Mother Ganga. At the water's edge, he removed the cotton *lungi* wrapped around his body and, wearing only a loincloth, slowly and with some difficulty, waded into the frigid water up to his waist. He remained still for a long time and then, without haste, placed his palms together and prayed towards the mountains to the east; he then turned and prayed south, north, and west, and east again. His shoulders rose as he inhaled and then he submerged his entire body into the water three times. Finally he was completely still again, with only his head and prayer hands visible above the water. The locals considered him one of very few true devotees of Mother Ganga left in Rishikesh. As I watched him, I felt immense love.

After he dressed, he began his slow struggle back up the steps with his containers full of sacred water. I followed and, at the top, watched him sprinkle his bicycle, first the saddle and then the wheels, the pedals, and finally the handlebars. As I passed, without breaking the rhythm of his quiet chant, he acknowledged my presence with a nod. I placed my palms together and he flicked a few drops of water on my head.

Back at the ashram, I heard the sound of buckets being filled in other rooms. I pushed mine under the hot tap and filled it with Ganga water. My ritual was quick, with my thanks going first to the electricity company because the power was actually working this morning and second to the little hot water tank mounted on the bathroom wall. Splash, splash, splash.

After opening the balcony door to the sounds and fresh air, I spread my yoga mat on the floor and thought of Dianne directly below me in the yoga hall. I could picture her and her classmates hanging upside down like a row of bats. She loves the practice and can't resist doing it every day. It's never a struggle for her.

Me? I'm living in Rishikesh, yoga capital of the world, so I had better do my bit.

Sun salutations . . . *Tadasana. Urdhva Hastasana. Uttanasana. Adho Mukha Svavasana. Chaturanga Dandasana. Urdhva Mukha Svanasana. Adho Mukha Svanasana. Uttanasana. Urdhva Hastasana. Tadasana* . . . Hmmm. . . I think I'll have an aloo paratha this morning and a nice pot of masala chai before I meet Rudra . . . *Savasana* . . .

Talk Four

As I got settled on the step, a half-naked sadhu approached me. He was ten yards away, with his right arm outstretched in front of him, his hand clasped as if clutching something. He glared at me with wild eyes and demanded, "What am I having in my hand?" I wanted to say, "How many guesses do I get?" but I wasn't keen to engage him.

"I don't know, baba. What do you have in your hand, you nutter?"

"*Everything*!" he shouted at full volume as he opened his hand to reveal a leaf.

"Jesus! Baba, you scared the living daylights out of me, man."

"Jesus is the Christian, who is truly being the great one," he said, with a considerable wobble of his head. With that, he continued on his way, leaf clenched in his fist, arm outstretched, heading toward the next lucky recipient of his infinite wisdom.

119

"Good morning, Rudra. How are you?"

"I'm well, thank you, Ray. It's good to see you again."

"How was your trip to Mussoorie?"

"Good, but very cold. I read that it is one of the coldest winters on record."

I told him about my encounter with the leaf sadhu whose hand contains everything. He laughed.

"You see, Ray. Pointing to this self-luminous oneness comes in many forms. The baba's message? There are not two things."

I told him that I was beginning to realize where I've been stuck for so long. He listened patiently as I explained how, while living in Japan many years ago, I had undertaken a rigorous discipline to play the Japanese bamboo flute for sixty consecutive days on the side a sacred mountain. I was trying to accelerate my proficiency on the flute and to learn more about the idiot who had taken on the sixty-day discipline.[12]

"Everything became clear on that mountain, Rudra. I could see, beyond a doubt, how my intense highs and dreadful lows were temporary—coming and going but not changing who I essentially was. It felt like a breakthrough at the time and I was satisfied that it was a real insight. Now I'm beginning to see that thought had claimed ownership of awareness."

"Objectifying awareness is a common error, Ray. Many seekers make awareness into an ivory tower from which to view

---

12   See *Blowing Zen*.

the world. They hear 'consciousness is all there is' and thought immediately makes it into a concept. It ends up as 'everything is consciousness and I am conscious of everything.'[13] With this reification comes the firm belief that consciousness is a witness, inside a body, when, in fact, what we call mind, body and world appear as you, awareness. However subtle it may seem, reifying awareness is still self *and* other. It is still duality."

"Yes, I can see how thought gets in on the act and claims to know oneness."

"Satisfied, most seekers stay with that belief and don't inquire any further. Others are waiting for an experience that verifies that 'self-realization' or 'enlightenment' has occurred. Only a personal entity could wait for confirmation of transformation. Regardless of how many times a seeker is told, 'This is not a new experience,' thought says, 'It is and you must do something to reach the goal.'"

"We've certainly come up with some very creative practices and paths to reach our goals, haven't we?"

"No activity or inactivity will manifest the peace that you already are. This is not for only a few 'special' beings. This is for anyone who has the earnestness and desire to look."

"I started out on this journey, Rudra, thinking there should be a better version of 'me' at the end of it. The idea of

---

13 During our talks, Rudra uses consciousness and awareness synonymously.

enlightenment or transformation of a 'person' is no different, is it? It just sounds more virtuous."

"Yes, quite. Enlightenment for whom? Transform into what? There are no enlightened 'people.' There isn't a 'person' to be found to be transformed or enlightened!"

We stopped talking as a group of men walked by carrying a corpse on a stretcher, the body wrapped tightly in a white sheet and covered in marigold garlands. Behind them a dozen or so more men followed, each carrying a bundle of wood or a tree branch on his shoulder.

"Ray, you have seen this aware-presence burns up all concepts, ideas, and beliefs. What remains in the ashes is real, and the real has no opposite. There is only irreducible, indestructible 'is-ness.' Your new friend the leaf sadhu was kind enough to share his wisdom. *You*, not knowing two things, find yourself as everything."

I nodded my understanding, wishing I hadn't called the leaf baba a nutter!

We silently watched a pair of shelducks fly low over the water. They have the same flight pattern every day.

"What you are, what love is, has no evolution or possibilities. Love is the natural state of all experience before thought has divided it into selves and others. Only thought imagines something having possibilities or evolving."

He took a deep breath and exhaled slowly.

"Ray, until there is absolute certainty that you, awareness, are all there is, keep drawing your attention to that which does not evolve. Keep coming back to your own obviousness, your own being. Not some future being, not some higher being or special being—just ordinary *being*. How it feels to be *you*, as you are right now. Everything points to *this* that you are because *you are everything* that is. Being everything, where could you *not* find yourself? Being everything, what could possibly matter about *anything*?"

The Parmarth Ashram clock struck ten times.

"Let me repeat. See that what you are is not dependent on anything. See that this indescribable presence is shining as its own light. Ask what else could possibly experience *this* but *this…* " Rudra held my gaze. "This is enough for today, Ray."

chapter nine

Dravindra Baba

An overnight downpour washed the ghats clean and on the sparkling Himalayan morning that followed, Dianne and I set off to find Tat Wale's Ashram. We could see the tall banyan tree in the distance, but once we crossed the Ram Jhula footbridge, we lost sight of it. Walk along the shopping street to the end, Rudra advised, and then cut in along the dry riverbed. No point asking any of the babas loafing around if they had heard of the reclusive sadhu. Yes, they would say, and then offer to take us—for a price.

We continued walking along the narrow road, leaving behind the small arcade of shops and busy street activity around Swarg Ashram. The road eventually turned into a rough, sandy path, which led us to a huge open space adjacent to the forest and river. In the distance, we could see the main entrance to the abandoned Maharishi Yogi's[14] Ashram, made famous by the Beatles in the late sixties.

A couple of mangy dogs slept in the shade of a bodhi tree, while scrawny cows roamed around looking for grass. Two half-naked sadhus squatted nearby, smoking hashish, their faded saffron robes spread out on the ground, drying in the sun. To attract donations they displayed a litter of irresistible puppies wrapped in a cloth. Behind them, three other sadhus lay flat on their backs "meditating."

"Hari Om, friend," said the one holding a large three-pronged trident, the chosen sacred weapon of Lord Shiva. Reluctantly, we Hari Om'ed him back.

"You are wanting hashish? . . . Friend? . . . You are having little money? . . . Friend?"

His companion, with long matted hair, joined in.

"Friend . . . Come . . . Sit . . . Come . . . Smoke charas," he hissed, as he crumbled a chunk of hashish in his hand, mixed it with some tobacco, and then dumped it into a conical clay chillum pipe. He set it ablaze and, before drawing a huge lungful, gave a loud shout, "Bom Shankar!" After a few massive tugs, his head disappeared into a cloud of smoke. With glazed eyes, in stoned devotion, he began chanting to Lord Shiva.

---

14 Maharishi Mahesh Yogi developed the internationally known Transcendental Meditation technique (T.M.)

Om Namah Shivaya, Om Namah Shivaya
Om Namah Shivaya, Om Namah Shivaya
Om Namah Shivaya, Shivaya Namah Om
Shivaya Namah Om, Shivaya Namah Om
Shivaya Namah Om Namah Shivaya . . .

The two sleeping dog, sensing something, came back to life, did perfect Downward Dog poses, and trotted to the path, tails wagging, to greet a tall, saffron-robed figure heading towards us. We Hari Om'ed the stoned babas and followed the dogs, intending to ask the sannyāsin if he had heard of Tat Wale baba. Anticipating the typical question from visitors, he spoke first.

"Beatle Ashram this way!" he said, pointing toward the Maharishi Yogi Ashram. "It is over there," he said. "Can you see it?"

All six feet of him was swathed in bright saffron cloth, including his bag and socks. Beneath an impressive white beard was the bright face of a still handsome man, perhaps in his early seventies. He was, by far, the biggest and most beautiful sannyāsin I had ever seen.

"Namaste Swamiji, we are not going to the ashram. We are looking for the cave where a sadhu called Tat Wale baba used to live."

The swami's eyes widened and he quickly mouthed all the English words that came to him.

"Tat Wale baba, I am knowing him, he is friend, my good friend." Dianne and I looked at each other in utter amazement. How could it be possible that the first man we approached declared himself to be Tat Wale baba's good friend!

Excited to hear the name, he pressed his palms together and repeated it again.

"*Shri* Tat Wale baba."

Hearing his pronunciation, I realized that I was pronouncing the name incorrectly. The sannyāsin made it sound more like Tat *Wala*, not *Wally*. Smiling at his happiness, I repeated Tat Wale baba, this time correctly. He reached into his large shoulder bag, pulled out a stainless steel food container, and said, "Please be waiting. I am getting the *khana* and coming back in one jiffy only."

We knew it would be longer than one jiffy before he'd return, but we agreed to wait. Off he went toward Swarg Ashram to collect the free offering of food that, according to Vedic tradition, must be given to those who need it. It would take at least twenty jiffies round-trip.

We perched ourselves on a rock away from the chanting sadhu and his comatose friends, preferring the entertainment of two pied wagtails flitting from rock to rock. The chanting continued until our friend returned, attracting the dogs' attention again. They ran up and jumped all over him. This time he threw each one a chapatti.

"Sorry, I am taking too long. I am Dravindra. What are your sweet names?"

We introduced ourselves and answered the usual questions—where we are staying, how long we have been in India—then, as if satisfied with our information, he invited us to come with him to his home.

Noticing Dravindra's slight limp, Dianne asked what was wrong with his leg. He stopped, pulled his robe to just above the knee, and showed us an open sore, obviously in need of attention. "We should bring Dravindra some medical supplies," Dianne whispered.

Before we reached his compound, we stopped at a tiny dwelling, a cave eroded into the riverbank with a small metal door. Whoever lived here could not stay all year round. It was at least thirty feet below the monsoon water level. Dravindra shouted something in Hindi, his voice drowned out by the sound of the rushing river. He leaned forward and shouted again. This time the miniature door opened and, with a bit of struggle, a man, smiling radiantly, hopped out dressed in a clean white *kurta* shirt and pajama pants. He had a badly deformed leg, which he adjusted with his hands as he stood to greet us. Coming from the cave, I could hear the sound of a cricket match playing on a transistor radio. Dravindra introduced Dianne and me as his friends and we exchanged Hari Om's. The man, Ganesh, immediately asked me if I like cricket. When I responded enthusiastically, he laughed happily and asked if I know Sachin Tendulkar. "Yes, I know him," I said. "*Ram Ram*," he muttered and placed his palms together in praise of the living deity of Indian cricket. Instant friends, he invited me to come around any time to listen to a match. "I will," I replied, wondering if I could fit inside his mini abode." Ganesh and Dravindra exchanged a few words and Ganesh reached back into his home and handed Dravindra a package wrapped in a banana leaf. We say goodbye and he hobbled back into his hole in the bank and closed the door.

Five minutes later, we reached Dravindra's hermitage, situated just below the abandoned Maharishi Yogi's Ashram and right on the Ganga. His hut, which is part of a small ashram, was covered with blue tarp, held in place by ropes, bamboo, and rocks for weight. We slipped off our shoes and then entered his hut, clean and quite comfortable inside. Saffron, the color that symbolizes Hinduism, permeated his room, from the cloth hanging on the walls to the pillows and bedding. Straw mats were spread across the floor and he invited us to sit at a small, low table. A framed picture of Shiva hung in one corner with a Rudraksha seed rosary hanging from it. Apart from a gas cooking ring, his bed, an altar housing several small deities, and a few sticks of incense, there was little else.

Dravindra seemed delighted to have company. "Go ahead and eat your lunch," we insisted. He refused and we were unable to persuade him otherwise. He wasted no time in preparing chai for us.

"I am cook and bodyguard of Maharishi Yogi." We understood this to mean that he once was. Without pausing he continued, "I am knowing Tat Wale baba," meaning that he once did. While we waited for the chai to boil, he talked nonstop about Tat Wale baba.

"Maharishi is liking Tat Wale very much," he said, wobbling his head and letting his eyes close for a moment at the memory of his friend. "Maharishi is inviting him to his ashram *too* many times. Tat Wale is very powerful guru. Word is spreading of the powerful mountain man with much *siddhi* and soon many seekers are flocking to see him."

It was difficult for Dravindra to explain all he wanted to say, so he poured us the chai, unwrapped the banana leaf package, and pulled out a handful of *Karah Prasad.* I was familiar with the thick sacred pudding given as an offering to worshippers at religious ceremonies. It is made of flour, butter and sugar, and scriptures are recited as it is mixed and cooked.

Dravindra placed an equal amount of pudding in three bowls and served us. My new cricket friend, Ganesh, looked clean enough, but we had no idea how long this batch had been sitting in his riverbank hideaway. "Eat . . . Eat!" Dravindra urged. The pudding tasted sweet and more than a bit musty, but we ate it anyway, counting on the sacred prayers to have somehow purified it. Dravindra ate his portion without hesitation and beamed as he watched us finish ours.

"Indian pudding only for specialty guest," he said, wobbling his head with joy and piling more into our bowls. When had Ganesh or Dravindra last entertained a specialty guest? I wondered. With difficulty, he got up from the table and declared, "Please be waiting one jiffy only." He limped over to a large tin chest and began searching through it. "Here," he said, returning with a pile of photographs and placing the first one on the table. Among the white-robed men I instantly recognized Maharishi Mahesh Yogi and Tat Wale baba before Dravindra pointed him out.

"This is Maharishi Yogi. This is Tat Wale baba." He pointed at a man in a loincloth walking next to the Maharishi. He was tall and lean with very dark brown skin and dreadlocks that touched the floor. "I am him, he said," pointing at an extremely handsome young man towering above the others and walking behind Tat Wale and the Maharishi. It was Dravindra—fifty years earlier, when his now-white hair was long, flowing, and glossy black. Behind the main group were several white-robed followers, some foreigners. In the next photograph, the length of Tat Wale baba's hair appeared in side view. His dreadlocks were so long that someone was carrying them to keep them from dragging on the ground. Tat Wale had a primitive rawness that clearly affected the others, who appeared to be spellbound by his presence. Dravindra pointed at himself again. "I am him." Then he lay down more photographs. One showed Tat Wale sitting in lotus position with his dreadlocks flowing down either side of him. A few more pictures were laid on the pile, all of Tat Wale and the Maharishi. He continued showing us more pictures, until the last landed on the table. It showed a group of stylishly dressed hippies posing in a row. Two men, five women, and an Indian dressed in white robes. "Beatle," proclaimed Dravindra. Dianne peered at the photo and began to name them. "That's John and Paul, Paul's girlfriend, Jane Asher, Cynthia Lennon, Mia Farrow, and I think that's Prudence Farrow."

"Beatle," Dravindra repeated, turning the picture over and pointing. Written on the back of the photo is the word "B e e t l e." I took the photo to scrutinize it. "I am him," he pointed to the only Indian in the picture. They were outfitted in the spirit of *Sgt. Pepper's Lonely Hearts Club Band*. What a rare and fantastic shot of two of my childhood idols. Back then I was fond of the Stones and the Animals, but I adored the Beatles. I'd worn the Beatles collarless jacket, Beatle boots, and, of course, the Beatle haircut. This phase lasted only until I was fifteen, but I continued to listen to their music and loved their use of the sitar in many of their later tracks. Had anyone ever seen this photograph? I knew that I'd seen most of the Beatles photos from their Rishikesh period, but I'd never seen this one.

Dravindra could see that we are thrilled with this photo. "Please, you are having the picture," and handed it to me. I'm tempted, but declined the offer and asked if I could photograph the pictures instead. He didn't quite understand, so we ended up taking photos of him, then him and Dianne, then him and me. Finally we took pictures of the pictures.

After the photo session—and the pouring of more chai—Dianne asked a few questions about Maharishi Yogi. He answered as well as he could. When she asked if this famous yogi was "enlightened," Dravindra didn't hesitate with his response. "He is having many money and one 747 airplane, Madam!" We laughed at the irony. When I asked if he remembered much about the Beatles coming to the ashram, he said, "I am never forgetting." Dravindra said that he was always with the Beatles, serving as their bodyguard and cook, while they were in Rishikesh. I mentioned that I'd read about "problems" concerning one of the female members of the entourage. I was thinking of Mia Farrow's alleged incident with the Maharishi.

"There is no hanky pankering! Too much the drug smoking only! But no hanky panky."

Even back then, it was no secret that the Beatles were interested in eastern philosophy, in addition to mind-expanding drugs, both which influenced their writing. *Sgt. Pepper's* is considered one of the most influential albums of all time, and it certainly influenced me. A track off the album, "Within you, without you," by George Harrison, first introduced me to the idea of "eastern philosophy." I loved the lines:

Try to realize it's all within yourself
No one else can make you change

For a directionless seventeen year old, the lyrics were quite radical.

With our questions exhausted, I ask Dravindra to draw a map to Tat Wale baba's cave. "Not needing the map," he said, "I am taking you."

A generous offer, but what about his sore leg? He waved his hand. "It is not a problem."

"When was the last time you were up at Tat Wale baba's Ashram, Dravindraji?"

"Much too long ago. Tat Wale is still living then."

Persuading him to eat his lunch was not easy, but he finally agreed. He would meet us outside when finished. We left, feeling delighted with our good fortune in this connection to Tat Wale baba. At the rocks by the river's edge, we made ourselves comfortable.

A parrot and a crow were fighting on the dusty grass nearby. The parrot would not back down; each time it escaped, it ran back into the skirmish for more action. Two or three crows were watching. There must be a nest nearby. Dianne threw a stone to break up the fight. They all scattered into the trees, squawking at each other until the parrot flew off across the water, the crows in pursuit. In the sudden quiet, I caught a whiff of hashish and the faint sound of the stoned baba's chant.

We lay down and closed our eyes. With Dianne lying beside me, lulled by the sound of rushing water, I drifted into thought.

... It seems so easy. Where is the difficulty in what Rudra is trying to convey? Where is the difficulty in remembering that *I am*—and I know that I am—whether there is remembering or not. *I am.* I understand Rudra's parting words now; I see that awareness is not dependant on anything...

Several minutes later, my voice broke the silence. "Do you recall how we first met in London?" I asked Dianne.

She opened her eyes and looked at me. "Of course, it was at that art show. You were terrible, trying to impress me with your non-existent art knowledge. Why do you ask?"

"How did it feel to be *you* back then?"

She pondered the question, closing her eyes. "That was such a long time ago. How can I remember how I felt that far back?"

"I'm not talking about the actual occasion, but simply how it felt to be *you*. Not your personal memories, just *you*." She stared into the water for a long time. I began to think she'd forgotten my question.

"*Exactly* as I feel now, Ray."

"Yes. It feels exactly the same. Only thought could say that there was another time or place."

"Yes," she nodded.

"I've spent most of my life looking for the very thing that is hearing these words. How foolish is that? Now I can see that the *sense* of 'I exist' is not created by thought. Thought can't hear or smell. Thought can't feel and it can't experience what I

136

am. It can't experience *anything* for that matter. Rudra is only ever pointing to the certainty that 'I am.'"

It flashed across my mind: the cliché of it all, sitting on the banks of the sacred river Ganga, talking about "finding myself."

****

"Here comes our knight in shining saffron, Ray."

"Hari Om!" Dravindra rejoined us. We stood for a few minutes, scanning the landscape and buildings on the other side of the river. He pointed to the ashrams in the distance. "That is Dayananda Ashram." His finger moved to the right, along the ghats. "There is Omkarananda Ashram, your living place." Then he smiled and shouted, "*Chalo*, let's go!"

"There are many ways up. This is quickest," he said, going back in the direction we had come.

As we approached the bustling shopping arcade, we could hear westernized spiritual music belting out from a gift shop. No surprise, it's Deva Premal, an American female kirtan singer. In Rishikesh, the music shops blast her CD all day long. If it's not Deva Premal it's Krishna Das, a New Yorker. They've worked-out the westernized notion of Hinduism and cater to it.

The arcade area was too narrow for cars, but a steady flow of annoying motorbikes zipped around people, horns blaring. Cows and dogs lazed around, along with fake holy men shouting "Hari Om" at any foreigner who looked their way. Young men, sitting on stools outside trinket shops, called out,

"Namaste, please come in and have look." One of the venders recognized me. We shook hands warmly. "I can't stop today," I said. With a head wobble, he waved me on. I usually stopped and chatted with him about his family and his life. He has two boys and found it beyond comprehension that Dianne and I don't have children. To him, this is practically against the law. He is one of three brothers. When I once asked him if he had any sisters, he said no, his father wanted only boys.

We turned right into the main compound of Swarg Ashram and wound our way through the pilgrim quarters and then onto a road leading uphill toward the Manikut Mountains. Soon we veered off the road and headed along a narrow wood-cutters' path lined with bushes. Dravindra used my shoulder to steady himself. Within thirty minutes, we were high up in the Himalayan jungle overlooking the holy city of Rishikesh.

"Ashram is only a jiffy now," he muttered, slightly out of breath.

Ahead of us, I could see a narrow, red brick structure seemingly built into the hillside. At the top of the steps, we found a small courtyard. The sign above the arched gateway read "Sri Tat Wale Ashram."

"Phew! This is it, Ray" Dianne whispered. We smiled at each other and then looked at Dravindra, who had slumped down on a stone bench. We joined him and took stock of the setting. A colossal banyan tree, which had wrapped itself around the side of the building, loomed over an improvised altar: an old, faded picture of Shiva in a frame, a tiny brass three-pronged trident. Facing the altar was a scruffy cushion made from folded pieces of sackcloth. Someone has been here recently. A flame was burning in a small dish of oil, beside a mantra prayer book lying open. The metal gate to the ashram was padlocked shut, with a barely legible notice: "Do not enter. Order of Forestry Commission." Dianne nevertheless tried to find an opening that she could squeeze through. Suddenly a sadhu appeared. Smiling and joining his palms in namaste, he greeted us, "Hari Om." Then he walked over to Dravindra and touched his feet. Dravindra leaned forward and touched his head, blessing him, and they exchanged a few words in Hindi.

"This is my friend, Ram Prasad. He is living here now."

Without fuss, Ram picked up the pieces of sackcloth under the tree and spread them across the bench for us to sit on. Then, settling himself before the altar, closed his eyes and softly uttered *Ram Ram, Sita Ram, Ram Ram.* After a couple of minutes, he appeared to remember his guests and stopped chanting. Dravindra described our situation, our interest in learning more about Tat Wale baba. Ram Prasad immediately lit up and told us about the great baba's love of deep contemplation and silence and about his sudden death. His English, it turned out, was better than Dravindra's.

Ram Prasad, Ray and Dravindra baba

He confirmed what I had read: On December 2nd 1974, Tate Wale was shot by a crazed man, jealous of the attention Tat Wale was getting. After the murder, one of his disciples took care of the property, preserving it like a museum until 2003, when authorities locked the ashram up due to a government land dispute. Ram Prasad explained that the property has been trapped in the court system ever since. On the anniversary of his death each year, many of Tat Wale's disciples still came to the ashram to pay their respects to this great yogi. Apart from that one day a year, the ashram, quiet with few visitors, was one of the only unspoiled areas left around Rishikesh. He pointed into jungle overgrowth high above the ashram.

"There are two natural caves up there," he said, adding that Tat Wale had been excavating many small meditation caves nearer to the ashram just before his death. He offered to take us to see the caves the next time we visited.

Dianne asked Ram Prasad if he had a key to the rusty padlock on the ashram gate. Unfortunately he didn't.

The sun was rapidly dropping low in the sky and Dravindra looked tired. It was time to leave.

We headed back the way we came, trying to memorize the route until we reached the Swarg Ashram compound. Here, Dravindra would go left along the arcade and we would turn right toward the Ram Jhula footbridge. Before we parted, he invited us to visit any time we were nearby. We agreed. Dianne wanted to come the very next morning, with antiseptic cream and clean bandages for his leg.[15]

---

15 The Laxman Jhula and Ram Jhula areas only sell Ayurvedic medicine. Allopathic pharmacies are available only on the far side of Rishikesh.

chapter ten

Tea and Biscuits

With the street dogs in tow, I walked to the chai stall opposite Flavors Restaurant. My four-legged friends' tails wagged eagerly and they took turns nudging my hands with their wet noses. They knew that a biscuit or two would come their way soon.

When I arrived, the gas burner was on and the sugared brew was bubbling away in the saucepan, milky froth and tea leaves rising to the top, but never boiling over. Raj, the tea master, made a big show of reaching into the bucket of Ganga water filled with dirty glasses. He grabbed one, swished it rapidly in the murky brown liquid, and held it up to the light, squinting, inspecting the glass as if it were a diamond. Glancing my way, to make sure I was still watching his hygienic performance, he turned it carefully, searching for evidence of fingerprints or lip marks. "Aha!" He found something, grabbed the filthy tea cloth draped over his shoulder, and started polishing as if he were a high-class waiter in a Monaco restaurant. The next step was every chai wallah's finest moment: the pouring. He held the sieve, hoisted the boiling saucepan of tea to head height and then, moving it up and down, expertly tipped his special brew through the mesh and into my spotless little glass. Nowhere in the world could you get such service for ten cents.

I held onto the rim of the scalding glass, took it to the shop step opposite, and sat in the early morning sun. The dogs were waiting, drooling as I ripped open a packet of biscuits. Then came the tricky bit—making sure to feed the alpha first and then the others—to avoid a punch up.

Ajna was sitting just around the corner from me on the same step. Sitting across from us, Laxman, in his late seventies and a fixture on this street, was muttering something as he studied his chai. One of the dogs lay down beside me, while the others, once they confirmed that the biscuits were finished, moved on.

Ajna, who'd laugh and poke fun at me whenever we met, dazzled me with her genuine smile. I had not seen her for several weeks. She looked well, wearing a flowery patterned dress, her short black hair neatly combed back off her pretty face. My young friend, who was four feet six inches tall, had no arms and one of her legs was much longer than the other. She spent her days on the Swarg Ashram side of the river, sitting on a mat, watching the world go by. She *never* begged, but strangers, attracted by her radiance, were generous.

The first time I met Ajna was on the boat crossing the Ganga. I was already on board when she arrived on the dock. The ferryman handed me Ajna's large canvas bag and then swept her up into his arms and carried her on board. Balancing on her shorter leg, she looked at me and indicated with a quick movement of her head that she would like her bag back. For a moment, I was bewildered. Where do I put the bag? I couldn't see anywhere to hang it. This made her grin and the ferryman laugh. Tipping her head several times and looking down at her shoulder, I finally got the message and placed the bag around her neck.

I wasn't sure if someone looked after Ajna, but I discovered that she was as dexterous with the foot on her shorter leg as I am with my hands. I've seen her digging through her bag, combing her hair, and drinking chai from a tiny bowl with no problem at all. One day Dianne offered her a handful of cashew nuts. She was delighted and, after directing her to put the nuts onto a small plate, she deftly gobbled a few, using her toes as fingers. Dianne gave her the thumbs up and Ajna held up her big toe.

I ordered another chai and asked Ajna if she would like one. She shook her head no. In my basic Hindi, I asked her what she was waiting for this morning. She laughed and said something incomprehensible. With that, a motorcycle approached and

Ajna suddenly screamed out to the rider. My body jumped into defense mode and the sleeping dog leaped into action, barking and attacking the motorbike. The man came to a stop as Anja rocked herself forward onto her feet and smoothly hopped onto the back of the bike. They raced off towards Ram Jhula bridge, chased by the dog. The chai wallah brought my tea. I regained my composure, leaned back against the wall and waited for it to cool.

Laxman shouted something to me. I looked over and he yelled again and then turned away. The shopkeepers all knew Laxman, who had been here when the street was only fields. He could speak a little English and, once or twice, I asked him about his memories of the area, but didn't get much more than elephants, tigers, and bullock carts to Tapovan. Sanjay, one of the shopkeepers, walked past and stopped to chat for a moment. He was wearing a New York Giants jacket and a baseball cap to match; his brother was living in the U.S. He announced the result of yesterday's cricket match between India and Pakistan and then walked over to Laxman. After whispering in the old man's ear, he looked at me, grinned, and walked on. Sanjay flicked a switch on in Laxman, who began blaring out obscenities that, I was told, were so awful they would make a rickshaw wallah blush. Laxman was notorious in Muni Ki Reti for turning the foulest language into a creative art form. I recognized a couple of curse words, but Laxman was going way beyond my Hindu cursing vocabulary.

Laxman and the street noise were too much, so I finished my tea in one gulp and stood to leave. It was too early for my meeting with Rudra, so I took a short detour to Sanjay's shop.

Sanjay was just lifting the shutters when I arrived. I thanked him for disturbing my morning chai time and asked him what he whispered to Laxman. He said the keyword that always sent Laxman fully *pagal* was Ganguly. Initially he would say "Sourav Ganguly is a rubbish cricketer." Now, just saying Ganguly set him off. Even Ganguly's nickname "Dada" was enough to rev him up. But Laxman didn't need an excuse to start ranting. When the shopping street was at its busiest, he liked to launch into a barrage of foul language. He could go on composing filthy full sentences for hours at a time.

Talk Five

Rudra was early. I could see him already sitting at our meeting place. He saw me and waved. When I arrived, he stood and placed his palms together.

"Good morning, Rudra. Have you been waiting long?"

"No, not at all. Only a few minutes."

We exchanged pleasantries and he gave me a few moments to make myself comfortable on the step.

"Ray, I have a joke for you... A disciple shouts to his guru on the opposite side of the river, 'How do I get to the other side, guru-ji?' The guru shouts back, 'You are on the other side.'"

It makes us both laugh. I'd heard the joke before, but it was still funny and had more meaning now.

Rudra, still smiling, asked if I have any questions.

"Yes, I do. I would like to keep looking at the function of thought, if you don't mind."

"Okay, good."

"I understand the thoughts that are about planning and carrying out daily business. I don't have a problem with those. Nor do I have a problem with the thoughts that we need to use to conduct our dialogues. I can see how these thoughts are useful."

"That's right, Ray. Thoughts that point directly to beingness are like using a thorn to remove a thorn. Eventually, we use the thorn less and less, until it is no longer needed."

"The thoughts that I'm still having a problem with, Rudra, are the toxic thoughts. The thoughts that want the story to be better or different. Thoughts that cause suffering. Sometimes they are just too overwhelming to see that there is no separation between the knowing and the known of them."

"Thought, Ray, could only be a problem if there was a thinker of them. When it's seen that there isn't a thinker of thoughts, they are like voices from another room. They appear as just a murmur or they don't appear at all. However, when they do appear, they are seen without resistance. I understand that it's difficult to look when there are strong emotions. Don't be concerned about the story they're telling you—just look at the raw feeling. Look at what you actually know and not what you think you know. See that the experience that we call feeling, and the awareness of it, is in no way separate. See that a 'feeling' couldn't possible be overwhelming."

"I can see that these thoughts and feelings simply appear, Rudra, but I still get caught in the belief that there is a choice to follow them or not."

"A choice for whom? The belief of a separate self that chooses is just a thought about another thought substantiated by a feeling. There is no 'you' doing the choosing any more than there is a 'you' choosing the green color of the river. All choices appear as thoughts. There is no separate chooser to be found."

I asked him to give me a moment.

". . . I see. No matter what the content of thought appears as, it's just thought questioning or commenting on another thought."

"Yes, well put, Ray. No one creating them. So, if choices appear as thoughts, like any other thought, in what sense could one thought know or control another thought? Can a thought know another thought?"

"Thought cannot know anything."

"Yes. Ray, what are you certain of right now?"

"Just this. Beingness."

"Yes, beingness is here and thoughts are simply appearing without a chooser. Ray, if there was a chooser and you could choose your thoughts, wouldn't you choose continuous happy thoughts? You'd never have a sad thought again, would you?"

"Right, good point but thoughts are just so damn quick, aren't they?"

"What does it matter how quick they are or what their content is. Thoughts don't belong to anyone. You know, Ray, thought is not as quick as you say. Experiments have shown that 'decisions' appear seconds before thought apparently makes the choice."[16]

"Interesting. Was the research done by a scientist?"

"Yes and, as you can imagine, it's caused arguments as to whether there is free will or not. Of course, scientists are looking from the point of view that there is a thinker of thoughts. Whereas awareness does not have a point of view."

"Most scientists wouldn't be willing to listen to what you're speaking about, Rudra. They want material proof—although David Bohm, the quantum physicist, did spend years with Krishnamurti and they agreed that they were talking about the same thing."

"The scientists would have to prove that there is 'material' first. They would have to find a substance that exists independently from awareness. Matter has never been glimpsed never mind found. Science tells us that awareness evolved from matter. Awareness is our actual experience and they are still looking for matter. Krishnamurti spent his whole life saying that the observer and the observed were not separate. That was years before quantum physics came to similar conclusions

---

16   Journal of Consciousness Studies. www.imprint-academic.com/jcs
     Benjamin Libet.

about the observer effect. Scientists have quite a job on their hands, answering what they are calling the 'hard question' of consciousness. Difficult to find an answer when *you* are the answer. They should first look and see if there is any separation between the knowing and known."

"Yes, When it comes to the debate about consciousness, science is curiously quiet, isn't it? Wasn't it Albert Einstein who said that all of our science, measured against reality, is primitive and childlike."

"Yes, but Einstein might have regarded reality as something separate from himself. Nevertheless, he was correct in his views about the current paradigm—science doesn't come close. If scientists won't listen to gurus, and who can blame them, perhaps they would do well to go back to the Greek philosopher, Parmenides and read him. Have you heard of this fellow, Ray?"

"No, I haven't."

"He wrote that 'to be aware and to be' are the same and 'thinking and the thought' are the same. Parmenides was speaking about the indivisible knowing and known."

The coffee wallah walked down the steps toward us. "Kofi?" he shouted. We took two cups and waited as they cooled. Rudra opened a packet of biscuits and offered me one. A dog instantly appeared and he, too, got a treat.

"I was speaking with Dianne this morning and she said that thought is like an illusionist that creates a world full of 'things.' Not a bad way of describing it, don't you think?"

"There's no problem how we look at thought, as long as we're not referring to a person in a body, who is a thinker of thoughts. Let's look at Dianne's 'illusionist.' Watch how thought creates a mind, a body, and a world. Like all good magicians, he has an amazing ability to convince you that the trick is real; and, as with magic, you become completely uninterested when you see how the trick is done. It is no different with thought. Once you see that it is sourceless and powerless, you lose interest. So let's bring the illusionist onstage, shall we?"

"He's ready and waiting, Rudra!"

"Okay. Now, please don't get lost in the words just because you've heard them all before. You have to actually look and see if what I am saying is true or not. Parroting the answer is thought's modus operandi. Okay. 'You are' and you can see the apparent movement of thought, right?"

"Yes."

"Your answer comes from the certainty of your own being, doesn't it? Despite what the illusionist says, you are already this aware-beingness and you need nothing to tell you this. The illusionist couldn't convince you otherwise, could he?"

"Never. He's just an impostor. I am and I know that I am."

"The only way he could convince you—is to create the illusion of a person, inside a body that is separate from a world outside of it. So, is there any separation between thought and the awareness of it? Be careful. Don't look at the magician's beautiful assistant. If you do, awareness will lend its reality to the dream character named 'Ray' and he will believe the deception. Okay. How close or how far is thought from you, awareness?"

I close my eyes and watch as thoughts appear spontaneously.

" . . . There is no distance. There is no separation."

"Yes. Have you seen the trick? Have you seen this clearly? You're not just saying this, are you, Ray? If it is just a belief then our magician will create the illusion of a person who will suffer."

"No. There is only thought, appearing as awareness."

"If there is only awareness, is there anyone to be found who could suffer?"

"When I look now, I can't find anyone who could suffer."

"Yes. And there is only now. Suffering is the belief that we are a personal entity trapped in a body, in a world. When you see that this is false, nothing merges, or surrenders, or comes home. There is no reabsorption of an ego. The personal entity trying to find peace and happiness and to end suffering is only an appearance, a show. You, awareness, know this show as yourself. You are complete. Nothing is missing. Nothing was ever missing."

Rudra stopped talking and leaned back against the step. I looked around at the scene and felt an intense wave of gratitude and respect for this man, who patiently kept pointing to what I truly am, day after day.

"So, Ray, here we are again. You can only find awareness. Tell me. What are you?"

A large brown and turquoise kingfisher landed on a rock in the water. Its huge beak looked too big for its body, its feathers impossibly vibrant in the morning sun. We watched the bird silently, waiting for it to dive.

"What I am—is all of this."

"Oh joy! Yes, it is that simple. Is there anything hidden from you?"

" . . . Everything is here, Rudra. Everything is I."

"Yes, Ray. Even when it feels like life's story is happening to 'Ray'—nothing could ever happen to everything."

"It seems so natural and ordinary Rudra."

"Why wouldn't it? It is like *not* having a headache. You don't have to keep reminding yourself and tell everyone that you don't have a headache. Nothing changes but there is the foundation of a deep peace that is not dependant on any 'thing.' Let's sit with this ordinary beingness and see that no conceptualization or special meditation is required for this to be just as it is."

We were quiet until Rudra broke the silence.

"Ray, why don't you stay for a while and look at all we've spoken about. Watch as thought gives birth to mind, body, and world. See how the illusionist becomes the knower, thinker, feeler, doer, and sufferer. See that in actuality there is none, no knower, no feeler, no doer, and no sufferer or thinker of thoughts. See that thought doesn't have a source. It's just an appearance, like the gold statue or ring. See that all we actually know is experience, which is simply you, awareness. See that there is only ever *one*."

chapter eleven

Worlds Apart

Dianne shook me awake. "Ray, someone's at the door." I looked at the clock. 5:30 a.m. We heard more knocking, now loud and urgent.

"Ray, are you awake?" I recognized the voice, so I jumped out of bed, pulled on my trousers, and opened the door. It was Yashoda, the vivacious Frenchwoman staying at the far end of the corridor. She looked confused and anxious.

"Ray," she said, in an urgent whisper, "I think Kishan is in my room."

I couldn't quite process why Yashoda, in her mid seventies, thought that the night watchman was in her room. I followed her and, finding the padlock gone and the bolt undone, pushed the door but it was locked from the inside.

"Kishan! Are you in there?"

A panicked voice answered, "Wait just one minute."

It *was* Kishan. "Open the door, Kishan. Now!"

I looked at Yashoda. "Why is Kishan in your room?" Too shocked to answer, she widened her eyes and held up her palms.

Only a week ago, a gang of monkeys had somehow pried open Yashoda's outside screen door while she was out and raided her room. Dianne and I could only watch as the monkeys, baring their teeth at us, had a party with her stash of goodies on the balcony. Now Kishan was in there. While we waited for him to come out with his hands up, he secretly made his way along the third floor balcony, mimicking the red-arsed monkeys. He climbed over the railing and along the dangerously narrow ledge alongside the building. When I heard the chai wallah shouting, I realized Kishan was escaping and took off down the stairs. Unbolting the front door and rushing outside, I was just in time to see Kishan jump down onto the street. I yelled at him as he sprinted past me barefoot with only his underpants on. The chai wallah and I watched Kishan disappear toward Rishikesh town.

"Why Kishan is running?" asked the chai wallah.

"He has an emergency at home," I said.

"He is having very big emergency and he is running home only in his *chaddi*?!" he said. This made us both laugh.

Usha Devi was called and within twenty minutes she and her driver arrived at reception. I told Usha about Kishan's half-naked dash toward his home. Stunned, we wondered what the hell had just happened. Yashoda explained to Usha how she had locked her door and left at the usual time for her meditation and pūjā gathering at Sivananda Ashram. Only today, noticing the full moon in the dawn sky, she had decided to go up to the top floor for a better look before she left.

"I came back down to use the toilet and that's when I saw the padlock was missing."

In all the years Yashoda had stayed at Omkarananda Guest House, she had never once changed her early morning routine until today.

Kishan, who slept on a fold-up bed in the reception area, unlocked the main door of the building at five a.m. everyday to let Yashoda and two other women out. They each departed at different times, so he left the door unlocked. This way he could stay in bed and if he didn't fall back to sleep, he locked the door when the last one left. Usha asked Yashoda to check her room to see if anything was missing. She knew exactly where to check. She picked up a brass statue of Lord Shiva, which stood on top of a box containing a small stack of 500- and 1,000-rupee notes. She quickly counted them and was quite sure that some were missing.

"I never count it," she said in her strong French accent, "I just take money as I need it. But I have always wondered why it goes so fast."

I suddenly understood how Kishan wore jeans that would cost two weeks' salary and was planning a trip to Mussoorie for the weekend with his girlfriend. Maybe that fancy new cell phone was not his friend's either. Yashoda's room had probably been his personal ATM soon after she moved into the ashram. Kishan had become so confident with her routine that he would just get out of bed, run upstairs, unlock the padlock on her door, and exit in a minute. Simple.

Binod, Usha's front desk manager, arrived and heard about the situation. He is habitually angry, but calm in situations that fluster others. He assured us that the master keys to the room padlocks are locked away and that only he has the key. I heard the word "duplicate *chabbi*" from Usha, as she switched to Hindi to speak to the manager. *Chabbi* means key. Kishan must have had a key cut. Of course. His father worked next to a key cutter's shop in Rishikesh.

Yashoda did not want the police contacted. Usha agreed. We had all heard about "encounters" with the police, so it was unanimous: don't get the police involved. Kishan's punishment would be harsh enough without a possible beating and extortion of presumed new wealth.

Yashoda was disturbed but philosophical about the whole affair. I ordered chai from the kitchen and invited her to join me in the garden, where she could talk through the morning's events. Yashoda was always laughing, as if she had found the secret to life. Only yesterday, we were in the garden laughing about how her *ayurvedic* doctor had run off with her money mid-*panchakarma* cleansing treatment, leaving her to cope with a very unspiritual bout of diarrhea.

Although Usha prohibited any talk about Kishan, soon all of the ashram workers knew what had happened and were brooding, worried about their own consequences. They distanced themselves from their friend Kishan, but I heard "duplicate *chabbi*" mentioned in hushed conversations. One of Kishan's co-workers told me in broken English, "Kishan is not good man. I am knowing him no more." He said something more about God and then crossed his arms over his chest and pinched both earlobes with his thumb and finger to indicate that God is his witness. A peculiar gesture, but rather endearing.

I waited a few more days until life at the ashram returned to India normal. Then, while Dianne was at her evening yoga class, I went to Kishan's home, not knowing if he'd be there or not.

I headed along the ghats in the direction of Chandrabhaga. It was dark, unlit due to a power cut. The embers from two afternoon cremations were still glowing as I passed by. I turned my headlamp on and took a narrow alleyway to a small shopping street. The area was teeming with activity and, without electricity, the harshness of the poor neighborhood was softened by candlelight. I switched my lamp to flashing to avoid getting hit by a motorbike and children followed me as if I were a Hindu deity, complete with third blinking eye. Kishan's home was down an alley, near a tailor shop, but there were three tailor shops and I couldn't remember the right one. I asked around using Kishan's caste name. They knew whom I was talking about, but they were not helpful. But their innocence gave me the lead I needed. I heard one of them tell a young boy that I was looking for Kishan. He acted cool and walked slowly away. The moment he turned the corner, he started running. There was no hurry—it was a dead end. If Kishan ran, he would have to pass me, not that I could stop him; he was a big lad. With some apprehension, I walked down the alley with no idea what might happen next.

The door was wide open and Kishan was sitting on the floor, shrinking against a wall in the candlelight. He looked at me, petrified. He was wearing a lungi wrapped around his lower body and a truck driver's vest. The young messenger was still panting after his twenty-yard sprint. There were two young girls in the room, probably his sisters. The three kids hesitated; suddenly the boy made a dash, followed by the two girls pushing at each other to flee.

Kishan's home was the size of a double garage and accommodated five people, six when he was there. I had no idea where they bathed or used the toilet but it was surely a shared setup, outside with only cold running water. There were two *charpoy*-type wooden beds, pushed together against one wall; a third was in the kitchen space and a fourth near the door. All were piled with blankets and clothes.

The ramifications of his robbery were beyond measure. He worked long hours at the ashram, but the job was not hard. He was on duty or on call for twenty hours a day. In the morning, he served as general gofer; at night, he was promoted to security guard. He had a small room for his off-duty hours, clean bed, albeit situated in reception, hot bucket wash, proper toilet, some money, the possibility of tips and friendships, and the same food that guests ate. He had responsibility and an escape from the cramped squalor of his family home.

I had got to know Kishan well over the years and would often talk with him just before he set up his bed for the night. His English was limited but improving. He taught me some Hindi words and we laughed about the day's events. Kishan told me about Indian life as a lowly paid worker at the bottom of the ladder. His ladder was not very high, but he was at least climbing one. Countless millions of Indians would envy Kishan, even if he did get shouted at day in and day out by Binod. Kishan was never well. I managed to persuade him not to drink the holy Ganga water, which he was misguidedly drinking to cure his stomachache and diarrhea. He had four hours off during the day and during this break would visit his family or stay in his windowless room at the ashram and sleep. Only three nights ago, he told me about his troubles and his dreams of being with his new girlfriend. Dianne and I had guessed that he had met someone; his newly styled haircut, fashionable jeans, clean shirts, and general tidiness gave it away.

He had not spoken of women before, but at twenty-four years old was thinking of marriage. Of course, her family wanted better for their daughter. From what I could gather, it wasn't a problem of caste, just money or, more precisely, his having none. His girlfriend wanted a home and a family and, before any of that, she wanted lots of fun. They were planning a secret weekend up in the hill station of Mussoorie. That was five weeks away. Dianne and I had offered to pay for a guesthouse for him, but he had refused.

Standing in his wretched home, I felt pity for him. Kishan got up, groveled out a few words in Hindi, and touched my feet out of shame and respect. He couldn't look me in the eye and started to sob. I gave him a hug and he pleaded for forgiveness. We sat down on the ground facing each other in a corner of the room, our backs against the walls. He still hadn't looked at me and I didn't ask him to. We were silent while the suffering took its course. Finally, I told him that he could get over this; that his English was decent; that he could move away and start anew. I revealed that there would be no police involvement. Still no eye contact, but I sensed relief. He mumbled a few words and then sobbed again.

"I cannot go to Usha Mataji," he said, terrified at the thought of meeting with her. Usha had his room locked; to retrieve his possessions, he first had to face her and his co-workers. Everything he owned was left when he ran. His new clothes, shoes, expensive cell phone, down jacket that I had given him, and a framed picture of his soon-to-be ex-girlfriend.

"I never went into your room, Mr. Ray. I'm sorry for making trouble." I knew why he said this. When Dianne and I would leave the ashram, we'd leave our key at the reception desk, often handed straight to Kishan. I didn't know whether he had entered our room or other rooms, and I didn't ask. Yashoda's stash wouldn't have covered everything he had bought.

Every day Kishan saw what he perceived as super-rich foreigners coming and going from the building. Many young backpackers were his age. Even if told that they'd saved for several years to travel to India, he couldn't comprehend their wealth and opportunity—and their freedom. He watched as guests handed over what would equal five months of his salary for only a month's room and board. At the main entrance, during an evening yoga class, he saw four years' salary in hiking boots and running shoes alone. Kishan saw beautiful young women from all corners of the world wearing skimpy yoga clothes, having fun with their boyfriends, and speaking kindly to him as an equal. He saw our world and wanted it.

Thankfully, Kishan did not tell me the outrageous tale he had told a co-worker and his friends: that he had gone upstairs to meet a young European woman. They had used Yashoda's room for privacy because the girl shared a room with a friend. His story would have appealed to the male egos in his peer group—common manliness, overcome with passion—much better than the truth that he was a common thief, robbing an old woman.

"What should I do?" he asked, whimpering. I offered no advice beyond repeating my suggestion of a clean start elsewhere. A deferential apology to Usha and to Yashoda would come with an interrogation and a minimum sentence of cringing humiliation. Usha was furious and rightly so. Binod would give him a beating and there would be a lineup to slap him. I had witnessed "instant justice" a few times in India. Most recently, while sitting near the ticket booth at the ferryboat landing in Muni Ki Reti, something happened between a man and a young woman on the ferry. The woman, who apparently didn't know the man, became distraught and started to cry. The ferryman couldn't remove the culprit from the boat, so he called out to an off-duty police officer standing on the ghat. The officer boarded the ferry and proceeded to beat the alleged offender. The upset woman joined in, slapping the man, as did two or three of the other passengers. After the beating, the man walked away as best as he could. The ticket collector next to me answered my protests with a wobble of his head, "You see, sir. He is not bothering young women again."

The sound of hissing from a nearby pressure cooker was my cue to leave. The tenants around us were preparing their evening meals. Kishan's family was probably waiting outside on the street for me to go. The electricity returned as I pulled on my boots. The light gave a brutal edge to the room.

"What will happen to me?
"I don't know, Kishan."
I shook his hand and left.

chapter twelve

Ram Prasad

Dianne finished her yoga practice early and by ten a.m. we were aboard the ferry, making our way across the glacial green waters of the Ganga on a brilliant Himalayan morning. We were heading back to Tat Wale's Ashram, to spend time with Ram Prasad and to explore the area.

An Indian family of five was making the crossing with us. Dad was taking a video of the scene, including shots of the two foreigners. The two children were excited and already throwing chapatti dough balls to the huge carp swimming around the side of the boat. Their mother, dressed in a gorgeous green sari, had just scooped a handful of Ganga water up and christened Grandma who broke into a toothless grin. Mum, Dad, Grandma, and the girls lived in Leeds and were delighted to hear that we were originally from Britain. I'm captivated by

Dad's broad Yorkshire accent. "Eh lad, thou wouldn't recognize the old country these days. There are so many new immigrants. Full to the brim it is." He shook his head English style. "They'll have to shut them doors soon, otherwise there won't be any future for these young' uns."

Ferry crossing River Ganges with Swag Ashram
area and Parmarth Ashram in background

As we landed at the Gita Bhawan ferry dock, a small group of men and women were engaged in various stages of their bathing ritual. One unlucky bather had just been caught soaping up in the water, a big mistake on this section of the ghats. He was standing on the steps completely covered in white lather, receiving a strident verbal thrashing from a self-appointed Ganga warden wielding a bamboo stick. I knew the warden well. One day, after stepping into a huge pile of wet cow dung while walking along the shopping street, I rinsed my boot clean in the river water. Ganga warden saw me and went mad, storming over waving his stick and shouting at me for polluting the sacred river.

As we clambered off the boat, a hairless pink dog, covered in mange, greeted us. He knew Dianne as she often fed him. The poor creature was way beyond petting, but she always gave the tip of his nose a good rub with her knuckles.

"I won't be a minute, Ray. I want to get some food for the dog."

As usual, Jetendra, the ferry ticket man, was sitting on his broken red plastic chair in the sun. Dianne waved to him and disappeared up the steps with her sick little friend following her. I went over to say hello and he held up his newspaper, pointing at the headline on the front page.

"One elephant is attacking one car last night on Dehradun road again."

In recent weeks, a rogue elephant had been on the rampage, moving through the neighborhood, killing people, damaging cars and property. The forestry department brought in a female elephant, placing her in a small enclosure behind a sturdy metal fence to entice and trap the bull. The first part of the plan worked, but he knocked down the fence and took the cow away into the forest. I sat on the low wall next to the fish-food seller and we listened to Jetendra as he read the article out loud in Hindi and then tried to translate bits of it into English.

"Road is closed! And, when open, only convoy is going through," he said, and then was interrupted when he noticed some people trying to board the boat without tickets. I saw Dianne standing at the top of the steps and said I had to go.

Once we find the overgrown woodcutters' path, we knew our way. Every few minutes, we stopped and listened for elephants and then pushed further through the forest. There was no sign of Ram Prasad when we reached the ashram, so we sat and rested on the stone bench after our strenuous uphill walk. In the distance, we could see the chaos of the main business and residential part of Rishikesh town, and below us, the ashram complexes were laid out in neat geometric designs with high walls surrounding each of them.

On our last visit, Ram Prasad pointed out a path that led deep into the forest to a small natural spring. This time we headed that way until we came to a massive banyan tree with thick woody vines and roots spreading in all directions. This was the tree that Rudra had identified as a landmark. An old brown blanket was hanging on a washing line. One end of the line was tied to a branch and the other end to a half-constructed shrine a few yards away. Someone had built a brick-and-mud platform beside the tree exactly where the morning sun hit. I recognized the platform from one of Dravindra's photographs of Tat Wale sitting on it in lotus position.

We could hear water flowing ahead of us and followed the sound until we saw a lovely, ancient-looking "one-man" ghat. Fresh mountain water was gushing through the mouth of a gargoyle. Flagstones lined the deep walls and banks around the spring. Tiny steps into the bathing area were laid with the same stones. Just above the spring was an altar with a stone *lingam*, its phallus shape symbolizing the male creative energy of Shiva. The root of the *lingam*, the *yoni*, symbolized the female creative energy, which alongside the *lingam* represented creation. Tat Wale had bathed and collected his drinking water here. I stepped in and kneeled to wash my hands. The water was freezing.

When we returned to the banyan tree, Ram Prasad was sitting cross-legged on the platform, writing in a notebook. His long dreadlocks were tucked into his white woolen hat and the morning sun was shining brightly on him. He looked marvelous wrapped in a purple shawl and faded orange pants.

"Hari Om. Come." He patted the brown blanket already spread out beside him.

"What are you writing, Ram Prasad?" Dianne asked.

He pointed to the first line of Hindi script in his notepad. "Ram Ram, Sita Ram. Ram Ram, Sita Ram. Ram Ram, Sita Ram." The same mantra is written over and over throughout the book. I'd once seen a sadhu on the ghats doing the same thing, scratching "Ram Ram, Sita Ram" with a sharpened stone. He was there every day and had carved the mantra along the steps for two hundred yards.

"Ram Ram, Sita Ram," Ram Prasad's eyes closed and he was gone. We sat beside him and fell into effortless silence.

In the Himalayas, the disparity in temperature throughout the day can be quite drastic. As the sun shifted off our bodies, the cold shadow prompted us to move. Ram stood up and told us that Tat Wale baba died exactly where we were sitting.

Dianne hung the blanket back on the line.

"Caves are up there." Ram said, pointing up a steep bank above us.

We followed him back towards the spring and took a sharp right turn onto an overgrown path that wound its way up into the jungle. He gestured for us to be careful as he moved through the bushes, snapping twigs so they wouldn't poke our eyes. We moved higher and then onto a narrow ledge with a steep drop down the hillside.

From this vantage point we had a panoramic view of the region and gazed at the new developments creeping into its surrounding hills. The forests were under siege by man. The view would have been quite different for Tat Wale thirty-five years ago—or for us, even five years ago. Just above us was the 160-square-mile Rajaji National Park, which helped to keep some wildlife roaming these hills. I told Ram Prasad that I'd once heard an elephant while taking an early morning hike. He replied that he often saw them around dusk and dawn.

"Here is first one."

The mouth of the cave, partially concealed with bushes and vines, was shored up with two sturdy branches. We bent low to enter and found a large square fire pit, carved deeply in the ground, with a pile of blackened rocks in the middle. Ram made himself comfortable on the dry mud floor, while Dianne and I sat on the edge of the hearth, our legs loosely crossed.

Sitting in a Himalayan cave with a man whose primary interest in this life was liberation, felt as normal as it once had to be drinking in a London pub. Since that experience so long ago in Samantha's nightclub, I'd been looking not for "normal," but for "extraordinary." I'd been looking for peace and happiness in objectivity. I was only strengthening the illusion, asserting its reality by struggling to get rid of it.

"Did anyone live in this cave, Ram Prasad?"

"No, this was only Tat Wale's place of meditation."

Dianne looked at Ram Prasad and asked if there were snakes or other dangerous animals around the ashram.

"Yes, cobra can be seen here. Tat Wale is living in cave with friendly cobra that he is feeding. Sometimes leopard is here also."

Ram Prasad ushered us out of the cave and led us farther along the rough trail until we could see Tat Wale's Ashram far below us. From here we began to descend until we arrived at another cave. Furnished, this cave was Ram Prasad's forest home. He removed his sandals and drawing aside the cloth

175

covering the entrance, ducked his head as he stepped in. The floor was made of red bricks and covered with old blankets. As did the previous cave, it had a central fire pit, but built properly, framed with bricks and mortar. A thick log smoldered in the white ash. Squatting over the heat, we warmed our hands. Ram gently adjusted the wood, adding a few pieces of kindling and blowing carefully to keep ash from flying around. Beside the fire pit, three charred metal tridents were planted in the ground. Hanging from the tallest was a tiny, soot-covered, double-sided drum, bits of tinsel, and a string of Rudraksha prayer beads. Ram Prasad unrolled his bed for us to sit on. He settled himself next to a small altar dedicated to Lord Shiva and then lit a stick of incense and the wick floating in a dish of oil. The combination of wood smoke and incense infused the cave with the unmistakable perfume of a Hindu temple. He removed his note pad and pen from his pocket and replaced it on a shelf behind him, next to his prayer book.

With all the power of his belief, Ram Prasad closed his eyes, chanted "Aum" three times, and then recited a melodic Vedic mantra to Lord Shiva. His sounds, amplified by the silence, felt timeless. This gentle, devotional being filled me with affection and as he sang, it felt as if the divine had entered the cave. I kept my eyes open as I listened to Ram Prasad's outpouring of love. A love that pours out of itself.

My mind floated back to memories of Grandad coming home after his long shift at the pit. Covered in coal dust, he is warming his hands and backside in front of the smoky fire. The tin bath is filled and waiting for him. He won't sit down until he's clean. As he mutters some old song to himself, Granma hands him a hot mug of tea and waits for him to sip the brew and say "Bye, that's grand, pet." The same routine his whole working life until "black lung" ends it. That night, peeking around the door at the bottom of the stairs, I watch as he gasps for air, as if he were drowning in our living room. When I can no longer look, I run upstairs to my bedroom and wait.

I hear the slow beat of footsteps coming up the stairs and then the noise of the bedroom-door latch. All Granma says is "Your Grandad's dead, pet."

Grandad didn't want me to work in the mine and was always saying, "Lad, if God had wanted you to go underground, he would have given you a bloody tail and a set of claws."

More thoughts, now of a small boy climbing out of the upstairs window, scampering onto the roof and along a brick wall, and then dropping onto the street below. Granma and most of the mining village are asleep. Those awake are miners, deep underground, and others getting ready to replace them on the six a.m. shift change. I wander down the long terrace, peering through windows into dimly lit rooms, watching wives serving their husbands mugs of steaming hot tea. I walk out of the village, over the fields, and onto the pit railway line, balancing along the tracks toward Hollywell Farm. The full moon illuminates my way. At the farm, I climb into an abandoned tractor, where I sit and watch an enormous white barn owl swoop in and out of the barn, feeding its young. My last stop is the red pit heap, a fifty-foot-high pile of hard ash. From the top, I look over the village at the long, slate roofs, silvery pathways across the sky.

"Om Tat Sat, Swaha, Om Tat Sat, Swaha, Om Tat Sat Swaha," ended the chant. Ram Prasad reached into the fire pit, took a pinch of ash, leaned forward, and dabbed it on my forehead and then on Dianne's. The symbol is a reminder to cast out selfishness and desire. We placed our palms together and thanked him. Dianne only knows one chant, the invocation to *Patanjali*, which is intoned at the beginning of her yoga classes. Sage Patanjali is known as the "Father of Yoga" and the compiler of the Yoga Sutras. She explained to Ram Prasad that she studied yoga and asked if she could recite the chant for him. He nodded in recognition and we listened as Dianne chanted, the acoustics adding depth to the solemn invocation. At the end, the three of us chanted "Om Shanti, Shanti, Shantihi" together.

Ram Prasad uttered more praise to God—Ram Ram, Sita Ram—and reached for an iron trivet with three sturdy legs, which he stood over the flames. I leaned back and relaxed against the cave wall, watching as he silently boiled chai in a small, blackened pot. Like Tat Wale baba, our friend had chosen a reclusive life; during the day, between collecting firewood, washing his clothes, and preparing his simple food, he spent long periods in silent meditation and contemplation.

Before we said goodbye, I asked Ram Prasad if I could visit the ashram again. "I play a Japanese Zen flute," I explained, "and I'd like to sit in the cave and play." He repeated the word "Zen" and paused. "*Dhyana,* meditation," I said, adding that the music I played was composed hundreds of years ago by *Komuso* monks and that *Komuso* means "monks of nothingness and emptiness." He nodded his understanding and told me that he'd love to hear me play. "Come anytime." We thanked him and he gave us each the gift of *prasad* in the form of puffed rice grains.

Dianne and I made our way home down the mountain and through the shopping arcade. The street was quieter now and, as we strolled along, we linked arms and chatted about our day.

"Excuse me. Excuse me, sir!" We stopped talking as a short, well-dressed man appeared beside us. "I am terribly sorry to be imposing myself upon you, but I feel I must inform you that it is not appropriate for couples to be touching in public in this holy city."

We immediately released our arms, apologized, and thanked him for telling us. That was our second warning in the same month!

We needed cash and stopped at an ATM. A young Indian man exiting the cubicle warned us that he had to do his transaction twice before the machine paid out. No surprise: this ATM was notoriously unreliable. I asked the security guard, standing at attention in full bank uniform, if he wouldn't mind entering the cubicle with us. He was dead serious as he witnessed our transaction. As the machine churned away, Dianne and I suddenly pressed our palms together and started chanting: "Om Namah Shivaya. Om Namah Shivaya." After the second round of prayer, the guard joined in. "Om Namah Shivaya. Om Namah Shivaya." As the machine dispensed the money we all cheered and laughed. The guard was thrilled that he could help.

chapter thirteen

Monkey Punky Gang

To avoid the black, oily smoke pouring off one of the cremations pyres, I had to take the long way around to Dayananda
Ashram this morning. The sweeper on the ghats told me that
they're burning a taxi driver killed in an accident the previous night on the Dehradun Road. The black smoke, he said,
was coming from the tires of his car. I had never heard of this
before. Like an informant, the sweeper looked around and then
held out his hand, hoping for a little *baksheesh*.

I stopped under the Sivananda Arch to see how Ram-Ram
was doing. Was he still alive? In preparation for death or
perhaps liberation, this man incessantly chanted the name
of God. "*Ram Ram, Ram Ram, Ram Ram.*" Crouching down
toward him, I asked if he wanted chai. He tilted his head, yes.
Ram Ram, Ram Ram, Ram Ram.

Old and crippled, he was left here to die by his family. They lived in another town miles away and could no longer take care of him. When Ram-Ram first appeared about eight months ago, he could just barely manage to get himself down to the Ganga to bathe and to use the public toilet. Now, the radius of his world was three feet; he could only drag his body far enough away from his sleeping spot to relieve himself in the gutter. He had warm clothing and food, mostly from Omkarananda Ashram, and I'd seen people give him medicine or a few coins, enough for tea. Some touched his feet for a blessing. The stall-holder next to Ram-Ram kept an eye on him and, at night, a couple of street dogs kept him warm and shared his food and blankets. I tipped the tea into his metal cup so it would cool, said *Ram Ram* to him, and returned the glass to the stall.

On the road, traffic was still light and, with no auto-rickshaws in sight, I started walking, checking over my shoulder, ready to flag one down. Within a minute, the familiar sound of a Royal Enfield motorcycle roared up behind me.

"I'm going as far as the Enfield mechanic's shop if you want a lift, mate." Thanking the young traveler, I jumped on. Five minutes later, I was walking through the streets of Shisham Jhari toward the ashram. Once away from the river, Rishikesh backstreets are more or less like any poor area in India. Here, however, the entire city is meat and alcohol free. There is no smell of butcher's shops, no wretched chickens crated up and waiting in the sun, and virtually no drinking or drunks in public.

In the early morning, the neighborhood, usually teeming with messy activity, was rather quiet. I passed a few dogs stretched out sleeping in the middle of the road, tired after a night's howling and fighting. I could hear the morning sounds of India waking up around me—a metal shutter being rolled up, a pressure cooker blowing off steam, a baby crying, a transistor radio playing Bollywood music. Amid the vegetable vendors pushing loaded carts to their designated places on the roadside, I saw my favorite chai wallah, Palu. He waved me over.

"Chai?" His jet-black hair was slicked back, still wet from his morning wash under the public tap.

"Yes, please."

Palu, who sleeps under his cart at night, was forced out of his own community in Bihar due to lack of jobs. He had been working in Rishikesh for the past four years while his wife, children, and parents stayed behind in his birthplace. Every week he sent home almost all of his earnings.

We shook hands and he poured both of us steaming hot tea. When I handed him a five rupee note, he refused my money.

"Almost I'm having a very bad accident this morning," he said in a familiar jumble of grammatical alterations of India-English.

"What happened?" I asked.

"For me this is lucky day. I am pushing the cart to here, you see. Every day cars are coming without caring for my safety-ness. Today two trucks are coming too fast. One is passing another one. I am in the middle of road, crossing, I am shouting very loud and using so many very bad words." He repeated the obscenities word by word, proving his anger. (Once you're aware of these words, you unfortunately hear them all the time.)

I blew on my chai and nodded sympathetically. His journey traversed roads without rules and vendors' carts came last—behind autos, motorcycles, bicycles, pedestrians, cows, and dogs—in the traffic hierarchy.

"Sachin! Hello. Flower. Please." Turning around, I saw a young boy laughing. It was Sushil, whom I hadn't seen in ages, looking taller and older, but with the same brilliant smile and mischievous eyes. Sushil was once a member of the Monkey Punky Gang and the only one who could bowl me out in cricket. He said something to Palu in Hindi about Sachin, and Palu replied "Good man" in English. Sushil was holding a ragged white sack filled with discarded temple and funeral debris from the river. I could see a piece of orange cloth, a red scarf edged in golden tinsel, and a tangle of marigold garlands. Excited, he reached into the sack and pulled out a wooden statue of the Hindu elephant god, *Ganesh*.

"You," he said, offering it to me as a gift. Everything he collected would be recycled and sold later today by the current crop of little flower sellers. Now too old to melt the hearts of foreigners, Sushil was a rag picker and helped assemble the flower offerings for the gang to sell.

"Sachin, come my home, please. Please. You come." His eyes were wide with excitement. "You see my *Nani*. Please, Sachin! One minute only. Please."

I knew that Sushil lived with his grandmother and two sisters, but I'd never asked where his parents were. Many of these children have no parents. Usually the mother has died and the father has run off or remarried, leaving the children with grandparents if they're lucky.

"Do you have school today, Sushil?"

"Yes, yes, no problem, later. Please you come."

"Okay, five minutes only," I said, knowing that a simple visit was never simple. I didn't want to be late for my meeting with Rudra, but Sushil was insistent. I thanked Palu for tea and said goodbye.

Sushil thought it would be a good idea if we stopped at the shop first to buy a bag of assorted sweets, which ended up being almost the whole jar plus a bag of milk. Just around the corner from the shop, we stopped in front of a tall corrugated iron gate. Sushil pushed it open with a bit of struggle, and we entered a small compound yard containing five or six dwellings. The yard was swept clean and crisscrossed with laundry lines full of hanging clothes. Two women were at the pump washing dishes and spreading them out to dry in the sun. They yelled out to Sushil and he yelled back something about Sachin.

Sushil's younger sister, Rajrani, saw me first and screamed "Sachin!" alerting the children in other dwellings. Within seconds, I was surrounded by the Monkey Punky Gang, new and old. They jumped all over me, trying to pry the sweets from my hand. I managed to hold them back long enough to open the bag and toss a few handfuls of sweets up into the air. The kids cheered and scattered, giving me enough time to follow Sushil into his home. We kicked off our shoes and ducked behind a black plastic sheet covering the doorway.

"This, my home Sachin. Best place!" He said with a proud tilt of his head.

Outside, the gang continued shouting and laughing, scrambling to get a share of the sweets.

As soon as Grandma saw Sushil she shouted at him—I recognized a few swear words in the mix—rebuking him for something or other. Sushil didn't flinch or seem bothered; this was normal behavior for Grandma. She sat cross-legged on the floor and resumed sifting through uncooked rice for bits of stone, oblivious about the foreigner standing in the room. Sushil addressed her in Hindi and then she looked at me and ordered Sushil to make chai. She waved her hand signaling me to sit. There were two beds in the tidy one-room house, but nothing you could really call a chair. I moved to the wall, so I could lean against it, sitting on the floor.

Sushil's sister dashed in, chewing one of the toffees. She was grinning, but acting more shyly than she did outside on the ghats. Grandma pointed to the large empty water container and said something about *paani*. Without argument, Rajrani took the container and went outside to fill it. Sushil worked competently at the gas stove making our tea, putting everything back in its place as he went along. The shelves in the kitchen area were filled with the usual steel cups, pots and pans, stack of round *thali* plates, and spice and tea jars. Stacked on the floor near the window were hundreds of the little leaf bowls that the children use for the flower offerings. A small altar over the bed contained incense, still burning from the morning pūjā; pictures and statues of Shiva, Ganesh, and Krishna; and, in a small frame, a photograph of a young woman. On another long shelf, I noticed folded clothes and exercise books. Three faded maroon school blazers hung on hooks by the door. So, the money earned and begged on the ghats was not being wasted. Two of the gang found their way inside and sat on the edge of a bed, chewing toffee, their faces beaming with pure pleasure from the taste. While waiting for the chai, I watched Grandma talking to herself and repeating Sushil's name. Rajrani returned with the water and three more of the gang. Grandma looked up, swearing about the *paani* again. Rajrani looked across at me, rolled her eyes, and shook her hand near her head, meaning Grandma is crazy. The kids all giggled. I could see that the children looked after her more than she looked after them. My grandmother used to do the same thing, repeating my name until the day she completely forgot it. After my grandfather died, she became worse. I began cooking more and more and was left to my own devices, which was both exciting for an eleven year old and a bit odd. One night, a huge thunderstorm was raging over our village when I heard Granma shrieking up the stairs.

"Get down here, bonnie lad, quickly!" She had forgotten my name by then. Thinking that she had fallen, I rushed down. Holding open the door of the cupboard under the stairs, she looked at me in panic.

"Quickly. It'll be safe in here," she said, grabbing my arm. Suddenly we heard a huge boom, followed by a flash of lighting, and she dragged me into the broom cupboard and shut the door. It was pitch black. Another boom made Granma gasp. "We'll be safe in here, don't worry. Your Grandad will be home after the 'all clear,' pet."

I'm not sure what worried me most, talk of my dead Grandad or her thinking we were being bombed by the German Luftwaffe. In the morning, I told my mate Terry my war story, which he thought was brilliant. He promised to come round with his warden's helmet and gas mask the next time the Germans attacked.

When I agreed to go to Sushil's home, I suspected that he wanted me to witness his family's awful living conditions. I was wrong. Sushil lived with a whole compound of family and friends who looked out for him. He just wanted me to see his home.

By the time I left, it was too late to go to Dayananda Ashram, so I headed straight to the ghats to wait for Rudra.

Sushil had wrapped the wooden *Ganesh* statue in newspaper for me and, when I unwrapped it, little marigold flowers dropped onto the steps.

Sushil from the Monkey Punky Gang

In less than five minutes, the weather deteriorated and I watched the landscape dissolve into thick fog, rolling up the river from Haridwar. The ashrams on the other side of the Ganga faded and then disappeared altogether. I had never seen fog quite so murky before. Then the river disappeared and a deep quietness fell over the whole area. I sat in utter silence. I wondered if Rudra would come.

Then I heard a muted yell come from the water and I shouted back. More voices, more yelling. A passerby stopped to listen and explained that the ferry had lost its direction in the fog, and the fast-flowing current was dragging it down river. I knew there were no lifejackets on board. In another two hundred yards, the ferry would hit the rocky rapids. The yelling grew louder.

Soon I heard outboard motors buzzing around and, as the morning sun burned off the fog, I could just make out the stranded ferry anchored about one hundred feet in front of me. I watched the passengers scramble onto the rescue dinghies.

Talk Six

Rudra arrived. Open and welcoming, he shook my hand and, noting the foggy morning, asked what the ferry was doing down here. I described the morning's events and we watched the last rescue dinghy tug the empty ferry back toward the Muni Ki Reti dock.

I'd grown fond of this articulate and generous man, and I told him, honestly, "I've gained more understanding from our few meetings than in my decades of study." I wanted to say that the missing pieces were coming together, but I knew he'd say, "There are no pieces."

"Yes, Ray, accumulated knowledge is a hindrance to the seeing that there never was or could be any separation between an imagined experiencer and experience. To see clearly that there is nothing here but experience is freedom enough. No more is needed. But please keep looking until the last traces of the misconception of separation are seen through. Do you have any questions this morning, Ray?"

"Yes, I'd like to ask you about *others*. I still have a sense that I exist independently of others. You, and those people walking along the ghats have different perceptions, thoughts, and sensations. How do *others* fit in with all this?"

"To whom does Rudra and these *others* appear? To whom does the character 'Ray' appear? You've looked and seen that 'I' and 'other' or 'object' are not two. For there to be separate 'others,' there would have to be a separate person, in a body, and there is not one to be found, is there? The experience of people, donkeys, dogs, mountains, rivers, Rudra and Ray are real, but with no reality that is independent or separate from you, awareness. They are 'made' of the same 'stuff,' to loosely borrow Shakespeare's words.[17] They do not have continuity or solidity in time and space. For there to be time and space, knowing would have to be separate from the known. We've looked at the facts and we find only experience—only you, awareness. People, donkeys, dogs, mountains, rivers, Rudra, and Ray are not always present, whereas *you* are always present. If you look now, you will see that what we call 'body,' which you were not aware of a second ago, is your total experience—and

---

17   The Tempest, act 4, scene 1—We are such stuff as dreams are made
     on...

there is *only* experience. Experience is present but it is neither an 'object' nor 'other.'"

"I see. Then thought gives experience a name and a story, a sense of others and of time, as past or future."

"Yes. Now let's explore your question of others. We'll look at the nighttime dream experience to show that 'others' are not actually real in the way we think they are. Of course, when I say 'nighttime dream' I'm not suggesting that it is separate or different from the waking experience. The nighttime dream might contain a river and mountains, donkeys, dogs, and all kinds of characters. Is any of the dream separate? Is a dream in parts or is it seamless?"

"A dream is seamless. There are no separate parts, just dream objects."

"Okay. In the dream are these 'dream objects' and the dream made of different 'stuff?'"

"No. The whole dream is made of the same stuff."

"Okay. In the dream, are any of the dream characters aware?"

"No."

"In the dream, is the dream character 'Ray' aware?"

"No. It's just a dream."

"Are 'Ray' and the other dream characters having an experience?"

"No. If dream characters are not aware, how could they have an experience!"

"Exactly. There are no characters having an experience yet the dream is real *as* experience.

"Yes. I see that."

"In the dream, is there any time, space, cause and effect, or free will for dream characters?"

"No. It only appears so while I'm dreaming. When I wake, I see that it was all just a seamless experience. None of the characters are experiencing anything."

"In the dream, could 'Ray' or do any of the characters experience suffering?"

"No. Characters cannot suffer."

"Yes, that's right. So, if the dream is real *as* experience, who knows the dream?"

"I, as awareness know the dream."

"Yes. Whatever knows *this* experience knows the dream experience. The nighttime and the waking state are one seamless whole that is known by you, awareness. Everything that we have discovered in the nighttime dream state applies to the waking state. Listen carefully here. With the belief that you are a separate entity in the waking state, things *seem* to be happening to 'Ray.' 'You believe' there are lots of separate characters running around, seemingly expressing feelings, emotions, implications, and problems. The peace-makers and the war-makers, believers and disbelievers, saints and sinners are playing their parts but, just like in the nighttime dream, nothing is ever happening to the character called 'Ray' or to any of the characters. Ray and others are appearances; thought stories that do not know anything. As I have said, people, rivers, mountains, animals, Rudra and Ray, are real, as experience, as you, awareness. All *you* ever know is experience. And the *whole* experience is self-aware. Experience never comes into contact with anything other than itself. Only experience knowing experience. Only awareness aware of awareness. You, awareness, are not dreaming. You are the dream. The dream is awake to itself."

"So if 'what I am' is appearing as *everything*, then anything could show up in the dream."

"There is no 'if,' Ray. You are all that is. And yes, anything can show up. You can appear as the lover, the husband, the griever, the cancer patient, the seeker, but nothing is happening to the self-aware experience that you are."

"I understand now what you meant, Rudra, when you said this is beyond the very idea of freedom. There is no one to be set free."

"Yes. *Who* would need to be set free and from what—a dream character from a dream character? What you are has never been bound, so it need not be liberated. *You* can never be known as a subject or object, yet *you* are never not known. *You are,* before a thought story tells you what needs to be done to find yourself."

"So, Rudra, even to say that you are the ultimate subject doesn't make sense. Ultimate subject to what?"

"That's right, Ray. For subjectivity to exist, there must be such a thing as objectivity. In other words, when we discover that there is no subject, we simultaneously discover that there are no objects. All you can ever find is *beingness. You* are all that is here!"

"It is such a relief to see this, Rudra."

"Isn't it? Now, returning to your original question, it is not a case of denying that others are here. They were never here as we imagined them to be in the first place, that is, as independent objects. There are no 'others' having experiences. There is only awareness appearing, as all that is."

"It feels so real, doesn't it?"

"Yes. That is because there is only the real. Have you ever known the unreal? There is no reality that is independent or separate from you, awareness."

We were interrupted by a Indian man and his wife shouting to us in Hindi from the top of the ghat steps. He was asking if we knew where Dayananda Ashram was. Rudra pointed into the distance and shouted back the directions.

"Rudra, how does awareness awaken to itself? There is no who, so what awakens?"

"You, awareness, have never slept and cannot fail to notice yourself. Awareness always knows itself."

We watched in silence as a group of mediators arrived and settled down on the steps about thirty feet to our left. They sat cross-legged in a long row at the water's edge, their saffron robes vivid in the morning light.

"Rudra, those sannyāsin might say one needs many years of meditation, along with some sort of method to reach 'reality.'"

"Reality and *you* are not two. Reality is *this*. Praying, being preached to or meditation won't bring *this* any closer. Having said that, isn't it wonderful to sit quietly, especially next to such a beautiful river?"

"When you sit here each day, you don't call it meditation then?"

"It has never occurred to me to call it anything. I simply sit here because I apparently enjoy it. The meditator, who is sitting as a motive to find reality is like a flower trying to smell its own perfume. *Who* will meditate and *what* is there to meditate on? The meditator and meditating are two aspects of the same thing. There is no more meditation than knowing what you are and being what you love. If the seeker is meditating, then that is what is happening."

I see the Muni coming. He looks in our direction and raises his purple hands high in the air in the gesture of appreciation of this glorious day.

"You know, Rudra, as I sit here, love simply appears for no apparent reason and feels like it is its own devotion."

"Yes, beautifully said, Ray. What matters most to us is love. This love is another name for awareness, and only what is timeless is praiseworthy of devotion. It can feel like there is a lover and a loved. But there is only ever *one*. Why not call it love? To be this love is beauty beyond measure. Love is its own source and reclaims all in its wake."

We remain quiet for several minutes.

"Could we call *this* God?"

"If what is meant by God is *this*, then why not, but if God means Supreme Being to you, it would suggest that there is a separate entity, which would know and worship God. God is only an idea held together by thought. . . What name to give *this*, which has no form, needs nothing, resists nothing, cannot be known as a subject or object and yet, is never not? Call it by any name you like—God, the absolute, consciousness, Self, supreme non-dual reality, *Brahman*."

Rudra placed his hand on my arm.

"Let's stop for today."

"Yes, okay."

"Ray, when you're walking around in this great beauty and it occurs to you to look, see if there is a *person* involved in this presence to defile it. Keep looking to see if there is anything that could possibly be absent in *this*? See that there are no others, yet respond to others as yourself—they are yourself. It is all *you*, and you will respond accordingly."

"Thank you, Rudra."

"Love has shown you that there is no path to love. Let that love shine into this apparent world. To be all this—is to love all this."

chapter fourteen

No Path to God

Jetendra, the ferry ticket man, saw me disembark and waved me over. He was sitting in his usual place on the Swag Ashram dock and passing marble-size chapatti dough balls into the hand of a huge, silver Langur monkey and her babies.

"Chai?" he called out, then shouted across to the chai wallah for two cups.

I was on the way to my flute lesson, but had a few minutes, so I walked over and joined him. As I reached across to shake his free hand, the black-faced female glared at me.

"How are you my friend? Where is your *Sita*[18]?" He liked to

---

18 In Indian mythology, Sita is revered for her self-sacrifice, courage, and purity, and Rama is revered for his courage, compassion, and devotion to religious values and duty.

call Dianne "Sita" after the wife of *Rama*. I pointed across the river to the yoga hall and told him she was coming over later.

Ram Prasad had invited Dianne and me to attend Tat Wale baba's memorial gathering this morning up at the ashram. We had to get there by eleven a.m.

The chai arrived and I sat down cautiously on the step next to him and the monkeys. Jetendra smiled, placed his free hand over his heart and said, "Hanuman."[19]

We raised our glasses to each other and took our first sips.

"You're hearing about Raju?"

"Yes, Vijay told me the day after it happened," I answered. Did you go to the funeral?"

He nodded solemnly and pointed to the cremation site on the ghats across the river.

"Many people," he said, "all the taxi drivers from Rishikesh, Ram Jhula, and Laxman Jhula."

"I'm sorry I missed it."

"He is owing many friends much money for paying the legal bills. He should have gone away to a new town in another place and become a sadhu, forgetting the problems of this world. Very easy to get lost in India."

Dianne and I had been friends with Raju for several years. He was the best taxi driver in the area—slow and careful and excellent company on long journeys.

---

19   Hanuman is a much-loved monkey god in Hindu mythology.

"Where did they find his body?"

"Near the turnoff on the road to Dehradun. He was spotted by a passing motorist."

Jetendra put one hand around his throat and, with the other, held an imaginary rope high above his head. The monkey reached up, pulled his hand down, and held it. The two of them looked forlorn.

A large number of pilgrims were getting off the ferry and making their way up the steps toward us. Alarmed by the crowd, the baby monkeys began to cry out. The mother looked agitated. I finished my tea, thanked my friend, and said goodbye.

On our way to the memorial service, Dianne and I stopped at a fruit stall and bought a papaya and some oranges to give to Ram Prasad. When we arrived, he was pleased to see us and carefully stashed the fruit to prevent monkey burglary. The rituals had already begun. We stood quietly as I scanned the group of twenty or so Tat Wale disciples. Only two or three looked old enough to studied directly with him.

After the formalities, we mingled with the disciples; the younger ones were excited to describe the miraculous abilities and the *kundalini* awakening of a guru they had never met. We heard that Tat Wale was either eighty-four or one-hundred-twenty years old when he died, but looked only thirty-five. One disciple reiterated Ram's claim of a huge cobra living in the cave where Tat Wale meditated and how the guru regularly fed it milk.

Ram introduced us to a spritely elderly man, Madhu, a disciple from the sixties, who had lived in the ashram for two years. I asked him if he had witnessed any of Tat Wale's special abilities.

"Of course, I heard many stories, but I can't speak of any such miracles that I witnessed. For me, I did see the greatest siddhi of all, the only one of any real value. I saw him transform many individuals from the pursuit of a meaningless life of plea- sure seeking to one of wisdom and God realization. Sir, I saw Shri Tat Wale baba give the ultimate medicine and cure people of their 'spiritual homesickness.'"

"Looks like the medicine worked for you, Madhu?"

Madhu's face became animated and he answered with fluency and eloquence.

"I came to Shri Tat Wale as a seeker after searching high and low. The very first spoonful of medicine was my guru telling me that I did not have to search anymore; that there is no path to God and I didn't have to make an effort to find infinite hap- piness and freedom from the miseries of life. My teacher told me very clearly that nothing in the field of change could bring me to this never-changing, eternal supreme. He said that God is always present and not disconnected from my very own self. I was just to realize this fact. I sat at my guru's feet, meditating on God's presence and received many experiences of higher states as proof that he is here. Now, I live in the knowledge of the supreme. Although we cannot see him, I believe he is always here."

Madhu paused when a young woman brought us each a small offering of puffed rice and reminded him of the group's lunch at Gita Bhawan Ashram.

"Looks like you have found the peace and happiness you were looking for, Madhu?"

"I delight in the knowledge of his existence. Once we have tasted his completeness, we cannot settle for anything less. Thanks to God's grace, I have tasted this great joy, so many times. When I am graced with his presence, my concerns are inconsequential."

The loving way that Madhu told us of his awareness of something greater than himself reminded me of what Rudra had said about reifying and taking a stand as awareness: "awareness of something greater is beautiful but the indivisible being of this is beyond words."

Madhu was interrupted again about proceeding down the mountain for lunch. For a second time, he invited Dianne and me to join them. We declined, explaining that we wanted to spend some more time here.

"Sir, Madam, it has been most enjoyable and a pleasure talking to you. I hope that God's grace allows us to meet again next year."

We watched as Madhu and the group followed their leader down the stone steps until they disappeared into the jungle.

Ram Prasad, said goodbye to his departing visitors and then invited us to sit with him on the stone bench beside the ashram.

I wanted to go inside Tat Wale baba's Ashram and, beforehand, Dianne and I agreed to ask for permission, if the opportunity arose. If Ram did not object, I would go. Here was my chance, so I asked, and he immediately said, "No problem. I will show you a way in." I told him that I didn't want to desecrate the area, and he assured me that there was nothing to worry about.

I expected to enter through a side door in the building, but Ram pointed to an extension on the roof! There was a small hatch; to get inside, I would simply have to undo the wire ties.

Even with the go-ahead from Ram, I felt nervous and asked Dianne if she would keep watch and shout if anyone came.

"Take the camera, Ray, and watch out for that cobra," were Dianne's parting words. I climbed in through the hatch and lowered myself down onto a short, narrow flight of wooden steps leading into a small empty cave above the main room and then down into the ashram. Halfway along the steps, I stopped and waited until my eyes adjusted to the darkness. The only light came from a small window, plus the gaps between the roof and the top of the walls. At the bottom of the steps, I entered a small room that looked as if its occupant had just left.

A tattered robe hung on a laundry line and a single bed against the wall was piled with blankets, with a pair of straw sandals nearby. Rags were strewn about the floor, no doubt where the cobra's family lived. Against one wall was a large altar with two magnificent photographs of Tat Wale: a large black-and-white print, rotting away in the dampness, and a smaller color print of him sitting cross-legged in the forest. On the floor in front of the altar was a hand drum, another pair of old straw sandals, and an open *Bhagavad Gita*, also damp and rotting. I took a photograph of the Tat Wale pictures and proceeded into the next room. And there it was. Tat Wale baba's tomb.

It was set back inside a small cave. I understood now that the little brick ashram building surrounded these two natural caves. The entrance to the tomb cave was framed with cement and pillars, one showing a painting of a cobra rising through the body's vital *chakra* energy centre. The white marble tomb had an inscription, written in Hindi, of his family name and the year of his death. In front of the tomb, planted in the ground, two life-sized trident weapons gave protection against evil.

Madhu said that Tat Wale baba had been excavating more caves above the ashram, and intending to build rooms for students to use on long retreats. When Dianne's yoga teacher, Usha Devi, first settled in Rishikesh, during the eighties, after the ashram was abandoned, she spent an extended period living in one of these caves. She found it difficult to live in such an open environment and was often afraid of the wild

Tat Wale baba

animals prowling around at night. When Usha lived there, she befriended a German woman with dreadlocks down to her feet, known only as Mataji, living in another cave. I've seen a photo of Mataji, and I suddenly realized that it was taken here, at this very altar.

Ram had given me incense sticks to light in front of Tat Wale baba's tomb. "Please repeat the words 'Om Namah Shiva' several times," he requested. I did exactly that.

Seeking a chair substitute, I found a wooden crate full of blackened utensils, kicked it to confirm that nothing slithered out, and then emptied it, turned it upside down, and sat in front of the tomb, which most of Tat Wale baba's followers had never seen.

Whether sitting on a barstool in a London nightclub or on a box in a Himalayan cave, all that is truly known is "I undeniably exist." When asked if "I exist" the answer is immediate. "Yes, of course I exist. *I am*, without doubt." The question does not need to be pondered and directs you straight to the answer. The very same question asked in different words, "Who are you?" pulls you into a thought story of "I": I don't know who I am; I'd better find out; I'd better go off and look for myself. Nothing is required to know that "I am." And this "beingness" has always been so. Not inside a body or outside a body. Only beingness. No knowing and known; they are one and the same. Nothing perceived can pull them apart. One need not struggle like a philosopher or a scientist, looking for its essential properties—it has none. I don't have to sit in front of a guru's tomb in a damp Himalayan cave to know it.

chapter fifteen

Water Seekers and Worshipers

According to the Hindu calendar, this day was especially auspicious for taking a dip in the purifying waters of Mother Ganga.

I left the sanctuary of the ashram and entered the pandemonium of an open ward. The road was packed with sadhus, pilgrims, beggars, hawkers, animals, and tourists, all jostling for space. Hooked onto every tree limb, power pole, and high vantage point were dozens of red-arsed monkeys, watching the show below, waiting for a ripe opportunity to mug an unsuspecting pilgrim. Traffic lanes were optional and every driver—of car, jeep, bus, or motorcycle—was leaning on his horn. Packed auto-rickshaws, designed for six, unloaded up to ten pilgrims from their tiny compartments. As the last passenger's foot touched the ground, a policeman, wielding a bamboo pole and blasting a whistle, walloped the three-wheeled death trap, forcing it to move on. God had surely taken his hands off the controls today.

Hundreds of pilgrims were already in the water, dozens more were undressing, some struggling to keep their modesty in the gusts blowing from the Himalayas. Others were drying themselves or sitting on the steps. A few women were holding their wet bathing *saris* up high in the air to dry, long pieces of cloth flapping in the wind like colorful banners.

Across the river, each ashram was competing for God's attention with loudspeakers broadcasting their longing for liberation. The loudest, a man singing with harmonium accompaniment, was brutalizing what used to be my favorite devotional bhajan.

I settled down on the marble ledge, two feet wide, running along the outside of the Omkarananda Ashram's annex building. The ledge, sheltered by an overhang, attracts many snoring sadhus who sleep outside guests' windows at night.

The German sadhu, who settled here many years ago, was organizing his few belongings. His makeshift home was shielded from wind by side "walls" of bamboo slats. On the window ledge, he had a small altar with a couple of books and Shiva and Ganesh statues.

Until a couple of years ago, I thought he was an Indian sadhu, albeit a tall one at six foot two with a large European nose and tangled fair hair. He wore the faded robes of a renunciate, plus a ragged cloth wrapped around his head, and his skin was deeply tanned and weather-beaten. Apart from serious-looking varicose veins knotted into his calves, his body was in good shape for a man probably in his late sixties. I'd only ever said namaste to him, but this morning I was sitting too close to get away with just a simple greeting.

"Namaste, babaji. Looks like another auspicious day for the earlier morning bathers." I said lamely.

He was pounding and shaking his straw bed mat, cursing in his heavy German accent.

"I put these sides up to stop the wind from bringing in sand. But I am not sure whether I should take them down or not. If I take them down, sand gets in. If I leave them up, many flies come in, to escape the wind. There are always problems. No matter what you do, there are always problems. Nothing is perfect."

I listened, while visualizing him in a former life, speeding down the Autobahn at 180 miles an hour in an air-conditioned S-Class Mercedes, trying to swat a fly.

"Problems, problems, nothing is perfect," he repeated, rubbing his scraggly beard.

Stumped by his renovation dilemma, he came over and sat next to me. I had no interest in asking him the usual questions asked by Indian tourists who want their picture taken with him. A few days ago, an Indian woman took money out of her bag, walked up the steps, and offered the notes to him. He politely refused. She looked crestfallen and a little embarrassed.

Beyond our chat about sand and flies, nothing more is said. He relit what was left of his *beedi* cigarette, leaned back against the wall, and exhaled. We sat in silence, watching India's kaleidoscope of humanity appear in all of its glory.

By nine a.m. the auspiciousness was over and the extraordinary dance of Shiva had returned to ordinary everyday chaos. The flies were beginning to gather around my new friend and he was growing a bit frantic. Time to go.

I could see Deepak, one of the senior members of the Monkey Punky Gang, in the distance. He was waiting for me exactly where I always met Rudra. I wondered if he was in trouble. He spotted me and bounded across the steps shouting, "Sachin!" Excited, he handed me a dirty plastic bag. I looked inside and saw five used syringes.

The previous week, I caught him chasing the girls in the gang with a syringe. I took it away and tried to explain the danger of handling used needles. He protested, whimpering and whining: he had found it on the ghats; now it was his. I knew he was telling the truth. I had often seen Indian tourists sitting on the steps injecting themselves. They were diabetics.[20]

---

20 The rise in income and living standards in India has brought much good to the country, but it has also contributed to a steep rise in diabetes due to obesity and poor diet (e.g., processed junk food and sugary drinks).

Later that day I bought Deepak a couple of packets of biscuits, reminding him not to touch dirty needles. His eyes lit up with delight and the other kids, missing nothing, came running over for their share. Before handing them over, I tore open each packet; their parents insisted that they sell back any gifts, including biscuit packets, and bring the money home.

My dilemma: If I reward Deepak for bringing me a bag full of syringes, I would become his regular customer for used needles, and he might prick himself or others. And what would I do with the syringes? When I took the first syringe from him, I asked a friend at the taxi stand where I could safely dispose of it. With a quizzical look, he took the syringe from me and dropped it into the nearest open storm drain.

Disposal of syringes had not made India's Top Ten list of problems yet. Everyday waste was already a daunting conundrum.

My negotiations with Deepak over the bag of five needles ended with him pestering me out of my baseball cap and promising not to touch any more needles. Then I had to dispose of the bag safely. Designated dumping areas—anywhere rubbish was already piling up—or official metal dumpsters were useless. Shoeless rag pickers and beggars, monkeys, dogs, cows, street pigs, rats, and birds constantly sifted through the rubbish.

I tried to think like a Soprano and looked around for a building site with wet cement. Then I had the idea of putting them on a funeral pyre, but the family probably wouldn't appreciate that. Meanwhile Deepak ran off, pleased with himself. In the distance I saw Rudra; he stopped to chat with the boy and pulled the newly acquired cap over his eyes.

Talk Seven

"Good morning, Ray. Deepak just told me about your arrangement. He's thrilled with his new cap."

"Yes, he's been on and on at me to give it to him for ages. I wouldn't put it past him to have collected the syringes just to barter for the cap."

"He's a smart boy. He may like it enough not to sell it on."

"For all my do-gooding, now I can't think how to get rid of these needles."

"Take them to the Sivananda Hospital. They might be able to do something with them."

I shook my head, picturing one of the hospital staff washing them in a bucket of dirty water. Once settled, I asked Rudra if he slept well, more to lead toward a question I had than out of curiosity.

"Very well, thank you, Ray. The rain woke me around four though. It was pelting down, wasn't it? Did it wake you?"

"No, I slept through it and had a really deep sleep, which brought up a question I'd like to ask you this morning."

"Good."

"I understand how—in waking and dreaming states, awareness is always here, but it seems to disappear in dreamless sleep. Could we go into what occurs during deep sleep?"

"Well, time would have to exist for there to be such a thing as deep sleep or sleep at all."

"You're saying that there's no sleep at all? You just said you had a good sleep and the downpour woke you up."

"Yes, I had a wonderful sleep. Ray, unless we are inquiring into the nature of what we are, what's the problem in using normal, everyday language? It would be ridiculous to speak in absolutist jargon during our conversations, wouldn't it?"

"Yes, you're right. It's annoying to hear statements like, 'Who is the one that sleeps?' 'Who is the one asking the question?' 'There is nobody here.'"

"Those questions and statements are relevant and poignant when asked in the context of inquiry. When they are thrown out without the slightest understanding, they just point to ignorance and confusion."

"Okay. So, Rudra, you are suggesting that there is no deep sleep at all?"

"It's not a suggestion. What we call deep sleep is only "deep" and only "sleep" from thought's point of view. Thought is saying that deep sleep exists and 'Ray' slept for a number of hours.

Wasn't it Einstein who said that 'time is only for the clock?' You, awareness, not being a state, have never slept. Nothing real ever sleeps and there is only the real. The unreal never existed."

"In one of the *Upanishads* it says that there are three states; waking, dreaming, and deep sleep, and a fourth called *turiya* or pure consciousness. . ."

"Yes, yes, it's from the *Mandukya Upanishad*. You cannot quote a single passage from one of the *Upanishads* and expect it to convey the whole of the *Vedas*. We agreed not to quote from other sources and to look only at our actual experience."

"The passage just seemed to fit my experience."

"The *Upanishad* in question clearly shows that *you* are always here—in each of the apparent states. In actuality, there are *not* three states or any levels of consciousness. The highest states of consciousness and the deepest *samadhi*, no matter how long they appear to last, always end, leaving you as you are now. There is only ever you, awareness, appearing as the apparent many."

Rudra waved the coffee wallah over and ordered two cups. He spoke in Hindi and they both laughed. He probably said. "Hey, this idiot thinks he goes to sleep at night."

"On waking, thought reports a blankness for a period of time. Only thought could presume such an absence. Can awareness, by its very nature, experience non-existence, nothingness? Have you ever experienced nothingness? Is there such a thing as nothingness? Has anyone ever experienced

217

nothingness? Thoughts, images, sensations, perceptions are not present but you cannot say that there was nothing."

"I can see that to claim there is nothingness is ridiculous. There would have to be 'something' to make such a claim or it would only be a belief in nothingness. But I do have a memory of an absence."

"Memory is no other than thought about the future or the past, happening presently. What could possibly be outside of this aware-presence? Is there something happening outside of awareness? If so, how do you know? Surely, anything reported would be a belief, a thought story. *You* alone, as awareness, know the whole show. Right here, right now. Sit with this for a while, Ray."

The pause felt endless as I held onto my thought, waiting to comment.

"So, Rudra, what we are, what exists, is no other than awareness, aware of itself. I see that."

"When you say 'what *we* are,' Ray, it's not that awareness is shared between billions of others. *Apparent* others and objects appear, *as* awareness. If you look at a painting, let's say a Constable, there are clouds, trees, a pond, cows in a field, and in the distance a cathedral. The light is magnificent. You sit and look, never once noticing that it is all paint. The scene appears only as an expression of paint. Just as others and objects appear as an expression of awareness."

Rudra went quiet and we both looked across the river: nothing seemed solid, nothing separate. The scene was empty of objectivity. I reported this to Rudra.

"Yes, Ray, 'empty' of objective qualities. Yet, nothing to do with 'emptiness.' 'Emptiness' like 'nothingness' is a concept that is never experienced."

"Yes, I see that. If emptiness was experienced, it wouldn't be empty."

"Science claims that there is matter, which is solid and dense, the opposite of awareness. This could be true only if there were a division between knowing and known. Science also claims that there is a 'person' who knows a 'world.' Yet a person or world has never been found in reality."

"Yes. I can see that only thought identifies with the body and a world outside."

"Right. Identification is for thought, not for *you*. The problem for the seeker begins with the belief that 'what you are' is located in a body. Mind, body, and world appear to *you*. *You* don't appear to mind, body, and world."

"And, what we call mind, is no other than thought."

"That's right."

Three women dressed in colorful saris walked by, their hips swaying from side to side like models on a Paris runway. Each had a long primitive-looking, curved blade tucked into the waist of her skirt. They were returning from the forest with huge bundles of cow fodder balanced on their heads.

"Ray, touch the step either side of you and tell me if there is the perception of something solid, dense, and inert. Tell me: is it not fully alive with aware-presence? Look around you. Tell me if you find *anything* that could possibly be called dead matter. Is there such a thing as matter? Or is there only this presence-awareness?"

Placing my hands on the step, I watched the women glide into the distance. All that I found was inexpressible, only aware-presence, only vitality.

Rudra spoke for me.

"Yes. Only the ineffable. Please allow me to repeat this. *You* are all that is here. What could be in opposition to *you*? Point to 'something' that is separate from *you*. Point to that which is not *you*. Let's sit quietly with the simple knowing of our own being—just the experience of awareness, being aware of itself."

chapter sixteen

Divine Madness

Narayan and I stood watching a tiny woman on the ghats struggling to withdraw part of her sari from the mouth of a giant Brahman bull, a trident branded on its hip. The pure white beast, with its great hump and long drooping ears, was passively grinding away on the cloth, completely unfazed by the woman's shouts and blows from the temple sweeper's long broom.

"Incredible India," I said, laughing at the impromptu comedy show.

Narayan grinned and assured me that there must be a God.

"How else is India possibly working?" he said, wobbling his head.

Narayan walked over to the great bull and, without hesitation, gathered up the hanging dewlap under its neck and pressed his hands strongly into its throat. The bull gave a bronchial cough that stopped his chewing just long enough for the woman to reclaim her sari.

"Good work, Narayan."

"Ray-sir, can I be having one minute only of your time?"

I knew what was coming. Narayan wanted to pitch his latest charity endeavor to me. In his early forties, he had a gentle face, childlike and kind. He wanted nothing more than to help people and was always full of imaginative ideas that would alleviate the suffering of man and beast. According to the local shopkeepers, Narayan was fully *pagal*, crazy, since he was a boy. Without fanfare or funds, he spent all day helping sick sadhus, feeding stray dogs, tending suffering cows, and keeping a section of the ghats clean. His last madcap idea was to collect empty oil drums for the homeless to sleep in: an India-style capsule hotel. When I pointed out that their legs would stick out of the three-foot drums, he said, "Yes, but their middle bodies and heads are being fully covered and dry." My favorite Narayan scheme was his idea of panning for gold teeth, rings, and rupees in the Ganga. Any big finds would go toward financing his next wild scheme.

When I first met Narayan, he said, "You are most welcome to my country, sir. Your very own great guru Jesus Christ is being welcomed here so many years ago. Did you know, sir, Jesus is living in one cave just a few short miles from this very spot we are standing. This one cave is being there for 7,000 years. I am taking you there any time for the praying."

This morning, Narayan looked troubled and unfocused. I had time, so we sat on the step with our backs to the great goddess of wealth, prosperity, and fortune. Narayan began his story.

"One sadhu is sick and is not getting better, Ray-sir."

I asked him for details.

"He is in the forest, just up the hill on the main road to Tapovan. It has been seven days and he is becoming the worst for the wear."

"Why haven't you taken him to the hospital?"

"Big problem is here. All the hospital beds are fully taken, so we are waiting until he is getting better."

I asked him to explain the sadhu's symptoms.

"One side of the body he cannot move and his leg cannot walk and his mouth cannot eat."

"Which side of his body can't he move?" Narayan grabbed his left arm.

"This side is not moving from face to leg."

"He needs immediate attention, Narayan. We have to go to him now. I might know someone who will take him in and give him medical treatment."

Narayan's face relaxed when I told him about 'my friend' the Dutch woman who runs the leprosy refuge in Tapovan. I assured him that she would not refuse this sick sadhu.

"It is an uplifting moment. I am most grateful to you, Ray-sir."

Narayan sprang to his feet, saying that he'd bring a handcart to move the sadhu to the hospital. There was no way we could push a cart up the hill. So, telling him to wait for me by the chai stall, I rushed off to the taxi stand.

Vijay, the driver on duty, had just finished polishing his white Ambassador taxi and was about to join his friends in a game of Ludo. I explained to him the situation and asked for help. He immediately agreed. We picked up Narayan and drove to the exact spot on the main road where we could enter the forest.

While Vijay waited for us, I followed Narayan through the bushes. It had been raining for several days and the trail was wet and muddy. After a hundred yards, we reached a make-shift camp where a group of sadhus were living. Two of them greeted us and pointed to a black tarp propped up with a short stick, like a mini tent. I peeled the sheet back and saw an elderly man, lying down, wrapped in a blanket. His name was Surendra baba, and he stared at me in alarm.

"We are here to help," Narayan said in Hindi. "You are going to be fine now." His face was drooping on the left side and he clutched his useless left arm with his right hand. Literally trembling with fear, he never took his eyes off me. I touched his face, arm, and leg; they were numb and ice cold. It was inconceivable to think that he had been lying here, exposed to the elements, for seven days, in this condition. I expressed my disbelief aloud. One of the sadhus commented that he had been suffering for much longer than seven days without any improvement. They had been feeding him and helping him go to the toilet, while waiting for the numbness to pass. When Narayan explained to Surendra that we were going to move him, Surendra panicked and his breathing became ragged. I tried to calm him and kept reassuring him that he would be fine and soon in safe hands. Narayan and two sadhus carried him through the trees to the main road. Vijay saw us coming and opened the back door; he had already spread a plastic sheet and a blanket over the seat. The men slid the baba inside and covered him with another blanket. I gave Vijay directions to Sivananda Home and told him that I'd settle up back at the taxi stand. Vijay waved his hand, indicating that it wasn't necessary.

I then broke the news to Narayan that I couldn't accompany them to the hospital. I didn't mention that I'd been barred from the premises by the Dutch matron. Narayan was dismayed.

"Ray-sir, they will not let me in if you are not with me as my official officer in charge."

I assured him she would not turn a sick man away and directed him on how to enter. "As soon as the caretaker opens the gate," I said, "walk straight in with Surendra and go directly to the hallway. Put Surendra down on the ground and tell a nurse to get Madam immediately. Then leave as quickly as possible. And don't mention my name."

I advised him to bring one of the sadhus with him, for help in carrying Surendra. The two men squeezed into the front seat next to Vijay and the taxi pulled away.

The next day, Narayan found me in Flavors restaurant.

"It is working like the clockwork, Ray-sir. I am thinking the baba is in truly big hands now."

I asked him to join me for chai. He refused. He wouldn't even sit down while speaking with me.

"Ray-sir, do you have one more minute only?"

"What's on your mind now, Narayan?"

"The cow and dog and sadhu in the street are feeling the cold so much these early mornings. I am wanting to build a fire that is made of wood to warm them at the start of the cold day. Wood is plentiful in the forest and I can go with woodcutters for the safety from the mad elephant and leopard."

I asked him where he would build the fire.

"I am building it next to the chai wallah's cart where the sadhus are gathering at morning chai time."

His proposed communal bonfire site borders the entrance to the rickshaw and taxi stand, and it's a covered area.

"Sorry, Narayan, but I think it's a bad idea. The whole place would fill with smoke and everyone would be forced to leave."

"No sir, it is working, I assure you! My only problem Ray-sir is I am needing one axe only."

I finished my chai and followed Narayan down the stairs and onto the street. We walked together along the ghats towards Rudra's usual spot. With the axe and bonfire already forgotten, Narayan pitches me his next idea.

"Ray-sir, you see, we—that is, myself and your good self—are taking the Christian tourist to the Jesus cave for the worshiping. They are seeing where this great man gained his knowledge. They are sitting or they are kneeling in the very same spot he is meditating." Narayan knew that I had an appointment so he breathlessly rattled off as many details as possible. "We are opening a dog and cow ashram with the many proceeds from this honest work that the Jesus followers are providing, Ray-sir." I shook my head, smiled, and wished him luck. He smiled back, cheerful even if I'm not onboard with his new idea.

"I have to go, my friend."

"Goodbye, Ray-sir. By Jesus's good grace, I am seeing you soon."

Talk Eight

After telling Rudra about my adventures with Narayan and the sadhu that had a stroke, I asked him if he's heard of the "Jesus cave." He has; he went to see it years ago as a young man.

"It's not far from here, probably about a one-hour drive east, following the river. It's very close to the Vashishta cave and ashram."

"Do you know anything about the cave legend?"

"No more than anyone else. The story handed down is that Jesus visited India during his "lost years" and spent time living in the small cave near Vashishta cave. You never know how these stories get started."

"Well, Narayan is ready to turn it into a tourist attraction for Christian visitors."

"Then you had better go and see it before it gets overrun with pilgrims. The area is worth a visit just for the views of the mountains and the Ganga from there."

A warm breeze was coming up the river this morning, prompting both of us to remove our jackets. I folded mine into a cushion and made myself comfortable on it.

"I have a couple of questions, Rudra."

"You still have questions Ray?" he said, smiling. "Once you see that there couldn't possibly be self and other, all questions are answered."

"Actually, it's not so much of a question, more of an observation. If awareness is all there is, where does that leave karma?"

"Exactly, Ray, where *does* that leave the concept of karma? For karma to be possible, you would have to believe you are a 'person' having an experience. Karma appears to be happening to a dream character and the dream character appears to *you*. When you look, you only find experience; you only find awareness. And you, awareness, are free of any cause and effect, which is seemingly happening to the appearance of the dream character called 'Ray,' who apparently suffers. It is not the dream that causes the suffering. It is the belief in the dreamer. Once it is seen that it is all a dream known by you, awareness, what is left?"

"What about death? What happens to awareness when the body goes?"

"Nothing happens. Nothing real could possibly die. Where could you go? How could the idea of death and the concept of karma possibly matter to everything? We grieve and we mourn the loss of a loved one, but we don't disturb the peace that we are. No one is lost to anyone. Love is never lost. The eternal gold appears as a ring and symbolizes a story of love, betrothal, and a life of happiness and sorrow. The story ends; the gold remains, as it always was. Did anything ever happen to the gold in the story of the ring? What *you* are was never born. So what could possibly be subjected to death? Neither ignorance nor illusion has ever happened to *you*. Nothing has ever happened to *you*. Death is a belief, like any other belief. Let me borrow another metaphor, Ray."

Rudra looked down at the lapping water, as if searching for something.

"There is a wave happily living in the ocean with other waves. The waves are moving towards the shore and they experience calm and occasionally stormy seas. The waves are unaware of the ocean and know only what is happening on the surface of the ocean. One of the waves crashes to the shore and disappears. 'Where did it go?' asks another wave. Now, you tell me, Ray, where did the wave go?"

"It returned to its source."

"How could it go back to its source? The wave is never separate from the ocean; it is only an expression of ocean. It *is* the ocean."

"It dissolves back into the ocean."

"No, an expression of the ocean never left the ocean to dissolve back into the ocean. The wave did not go anywhere nor could it go anywhere. It didn't go to a *bardo*[21] or to heaven or hell, or reshape itself into something else. It wasn't reincarnated into a higher or lower wave. The wave didn't go to a better place. It didn't go anywhere. The wave is a beautiful appearance of ocean, but never is anything else but ocean. The ocean is all there is. In our metaphor, the ocean is one. Where can ocean go when it is all that is? Where can oneness go when it is all that is? Where could *you* go when you are all that is?"

"Yes. I understand. The imaginary seeker is looking for a source that could exist only if there were two things. Thoughts like 'I have not arrived, I have not realized' have no meaning. Oneness needs no meaning nor is it meaningless."

"Halleluiah, Ray. Meaning and meaningless are only for the imagined self. The appearance of a ring is always gold. The appearance of a pot is always clay. The appearance of thought is the same as any other appearance. Oneness is only ever one. *You*, being all there is, have no source. See this, and you see that there is no death; see that there is no death, and you see that there is no birth. Seeing that there is no death ends fear and even the possibility that there could exist anyone who could have fear."

"It sounds like the wave is moving in time and space, Rudra, but it can't be so. Time does not exist."

---

21 In Tibetan Buddhism, *bardo* is a state of existence between death and rebirth.

"Yes. Time and space are no other than the products of mind, which as we have seen are nothing but thoughts. What *you* are is timeless. What thought says is time-bound. So, the waves never move through space and time. They are only expressions of ocean. The ocean is only wave-ing, so to speak. The appearance of a wave is always only ocean. The appearance of 'Ray' is always only awareness. What could possibly die?"

A hungry female dog approached us, sniffing around for food. She surely had a litter of puppies somewhere. Her nipples were hanging low and she was terribly thin. Rudra stopped talking for a moment, pulled out a packet of biscuits from his coat pocket, and fed them to her. With the last few crumbs licked up, we watched her slowly walk away, exhausted.

"While I was walking with Narayan, I was reminded of what you'd said about this not being the end of compassion. The experience of compassion seems to appear more powerful than ever now. There's no longer a sense of doer who feels that he should act out of pity or sympathy or duty. It's more of a deeply shared sorrow—not one person feeling sorry for another person. It doesn't mean that there's no action."

"Yes. Compassion appears with an unlimited response. When it is seen that you are not in a body and that the other is yourself, compassion and joy appear naturally. Being simply being. Love only loving. True peace and harmony with the apparent world and others is realizing that you are *one*—without a second."

chapter seventeen

Gurus, Mystics and Saints

Binod, the Omkarananda guesthouse manager, and I watched a noisy procession making its way past our building, toward the ferry dock. Hundreds of sadhus, laypeople, and monks were walking behind a thoroughly decorated pickup truck. Marigolds engulfed the vehicle, which carried, in the back, an important-looking holy man. He was sitting in lotus position and, around his neck, were layer upon layer of jasmine, rose, and marigold garlands.

A ragtag group of marching musicians in baggy brown uniforms trimmed in gold was blasting out a tune. The drummer was trying to set the tempo, but it sounded more like he was building a shed. Binod explained that the man sitting in the back of the truck died last night. He was a great saint from one of the oldest ashrams in Rishikesh. He would have a water burial.

Some of the Monkey Punky Gang

Dianne left the yoga hall to check out the commotion, and we decided to join the crowd at the dock and watch this unusual ritual. When we arrived at the ghats, some of the Monkey Punky Gang were sitting on the steps closest to the wharf. They squealed when they saw us and waved for us to join them. We pushed through the crowd and the children shifted along to make space for us. We all grabbed hands into a big pile and they shouted "Monkey Punky!" Rajrani wore a red-and-gold tinsel shawl over her head and pulled Dianne close enough to cover her head, too. Rajrani giggled, bubbling over with affection and joy.

We recognized several locally eminent saints, who were the heads of ashrams. Considered to be "realized" beings, they were already on a garland-covered ferry, preparing for the arrival of the body.

Five monks carefully removed the corpse from the truck and carried it down the ghat steps to the ferry. On the riverbank, fifty or more monks were chanting scriptures aloud nonstop. On the ferry, the monks lifted the body into a large square wooden crate lined with large rocks. Through slats in the crate we could see the deceased guru still upright. Without ceremony, each of the eminent saints, in turn, leaned into the crate and began to cut and strip away the robes and flowers covering the corpse. Once the body was naked, they bathed it in Ganga water. Then the ferrymen placed more rocks into the container and nailed wooden slats across the top to keep the body from floating to the surface of the river. The prayers got louder and, with one tug, the outboard motor sputtered and rumbled into life. On the river, the ferry's movement against the strong current was almost undetectable as it passed under the Ram Jhula suspension bridge. At the deepest part of the river, the monks cast out the guru's belongings. An orange robe fanned out across the water, joined by a shawl and garlands of flowers. As the ferrymen pushed the heavy crate into the river, the boat tilted dangerously for a moment and then recovered. It would take only three days for the fish to clean all the flesh from the bones.

As we walked back to the ashram, the children shouted goodbye and raced off downriver, eager to collect the saintly possessions and tomorrow's flower offerings. The jasmine wouldn't last but the marigolds and rosebuds would keep.

Dianne returned to the yoga hall to finish her morning practice while I went downstairs to meet Rudra. He was already sitting in the garden.

An Indian couple from Delhi, looking rather wet, and bedraggled, stood at the wrought iron gate leading off the ghat steps into the Omkarananda garden. They saw us and called for help.

"Could you open the gate for us, please? It seems to be stuck." With a strong push, it scraped open.

"We are so grateful to you. We were bathing when the procession arrived and then I couldn't find my towel and my husband lost his spectacles." He held them up, relieved to have found them. "I'm so glad to be back in this little sanctuary. Stepping in here, it feels rather like we've left India behind, doesn't it?" As they dripped their way into the building, I laughed and agreed. Surrounding the garden is a shoulder-high yellow stonewall. On top of the wall is a decorative wrought iron fence, a border between chaos and respite.

Under Usha's watchful eye, the staff has created two small lawns and a garden filled with flowers, tropical plants, and statues of Hindu divinities. The poinsettia, hibiscus, and rose bushes were in bloom, attracting many tiny songbirds and butterflies that flitted from shrub to shrub throughout the day. Standing tall, close to the yoga hall window was an impressive palm tree. Safe from the street dogs, the garden also housed a crippled monkey, who napped on the cement wall near the kitchen door and liked to visit from time to time. Her hind legs must have been injured at some time, since she walked only on her hands. A skinny feral cat hunted for mice and slept without fear in the warm flowerbeds during the day. Under a green canopy, two tables were perfectly sheltered from the noonday sun: an idyllic place to have lunch.

Dianne knocked on the yoga hall window above us and waved. She would join us in the garden for lunch when she finished her practice. It was Dianne's idea to invite Rudra to the ashram, where the food is *sattvic*[22] and simple and the setting pleasant. Kusum, the lunchtime cook, brought out a pot of chai with a plate of biscuits on a tray as a special treat for my guest.

---

22 Sattvic diet means eating in moderation food that is pure, essential, natural, energy containing, clean, conscious, and without meat, garlic, or onions.

She even used china cups. Rudra and Kusum exchanged words in Hindi and laughed together before she left.

"Tea and biscuits in the garden. This is very English, I must say, Ray."

As I poured the tea, half went in the cup, half went on the tray, and some of it leaked out from where the spout meets the pot. I had forgotten for a moment the knack to pouring from an Indian teapot. First, you must pry the lid off with a teaspoon and then, bypassing the spout altogether, tip and pour fast with confidence.

"A gentle reminder, Rudra, that we're not in England."

Rudra's back was facing the Ganga, so he couldn't see the Monkey Punky Gang arrive and peek at us through the railings. All that was visible were their cheeky grinning faces and arms reaching up and poking through the bars. Each time I looked up, they acted out, silently, their pleading, hungry beggar look: brows knitted together, pointing at the biscuits and putting their bunched fingers to their mouths. They couldn't keep quiet for long and soon burst into fits of giggles before they ran off shouting and laughing.

"This reminds me of Sunday afternoons with my parents in our garden," Rudra commented, after tasting the tea. "Very nice. Quite an improvement on drinking Ram Singh's sticky coffee out of a plastic cup, wouldn't you say?"

With the mention of his parents, I take the opportunity to ask him more about himself and his upbringing.

Talk Nine

His father was British, from Oxford, and his mother was Indian.

"My father was a missionary," he continued.

"An English missionary. That must have been an interesting childhood, Rudra."

"Yes, it certainly was. My father came to India as a young man and, once he married and started a family, never returned to England. He and my mother were very happy in Mussoorie. They both loved the mountains and the beautiful nature walks up there. He named me John but my mother always called me Rudra, after her father."

"So you were brought up and educated in the Christian faith?"

"Yes, very much so. When I was old enough, my parents had me incarcerated in an English boarding school first in Darjeeling and then back in Mussoorie. My father hoped I would follow in his footsteps and become a missionary, but eventually my belief in the Christian doctrine wavered."

"Was that difficult for you at the time?"

"Boarding school or the Christian faith?"

"Both."

"Well, I never liked being away from home and my mother and, as I got older, I found myself getting into trouble at school. I was constantly drawn into philosophical debates questioning everything to do with literature, the great philosophers, science, and especially the gospels. I'm sure that my Religious Instruction teacher used to dread seeing my hand go up in the classroom. My interest in Christianity came under intense scrutiny when I saw that my educators' beliefs stopped any possibility of an open inquiry. By the time I was about fifteen, I had a profound sense that there was a discrepancy between what I was being taught about Jesus' message and what Jesus was actually saying. My teachers weren't open to any new interpretations of the gospels, that's for sure. We just had to memorize what we were told, parrot fashion."

"Yes, my school was the same. I remember reading something in the Christian teachings where Jesus talked about giving direct knowledge to his disciples, but not to the masses."

"Yes, that's right. It's in Matthew.[23] He said, "Why do you speak to the people in parables?" Jesus said, "Because the

---

23   13:10-11.

knowledge of the Kingdom of Heaven is given to you, but not to them." There are similar passages confirming this in the gospels of Mark[24] and Luke.[25] The teachings are referred to as the 'secret mysteries of the kingdom of heaven.' Some of the early Christians believed that there were certain gospels that revealed secret messages of the true knowledge."

"Did you study these 'secret' teachings as a young man?"

"Yes. I was fascinated by them."

"Did you have any breakthroughs?"

"Yes, I did. I was reading a passage from Luke for the umpteenth time: 'You won't be able to say, behold, here it is, or behold, it's over there, for the kingdom of God is within.'[26] Jesus was speaking to those who believed in duality. He was preaching to people who believed that they were 'inside' a body looking 'outside' at a world. I was already questioning the validity of a separation of a 'within and without.' I was questioning whether consciousness was in a container at all. I remember getting into trouble for writing in my textbook that 'all this is God's dream and I am but a dreamer.' Of course, I hadn't realized then that awareness and the dream are not two."

"'All things were made by him.' Do you know that passage, Rudra?"

---

24 4: 11.

25 8:9-10.

26 Luke 17:20:21.

"Yes. It continues, 'and without him was not anything made that was made.' It's from John.[27] It still suggests that there is a subject separate from object."

"Yes, I see that, but if you replace 'by him' with 'of consciousness,' it's basically the idea of one—without a second, isn't it?"

"Yes. Consciousness is all there is. That is exactly how I was beginning to understand what I was reading, but I had to keep my findings to myself. It would have been blasphemy for me to speak about such things to my father or anyone back then."

"That must have been difficult for you."

"Yes, I would have been considered a heretic if I had voiced those views. Such interpretations could get you ostracized back in those days. Speaking of heresy, Ray, you've probably heard of the Christian mystic, Meister Eckhart?"

"Yes. I read some of his work while I was looking at books on the non-dual Christian perspective."

"Unfortunately, I didn't find Eckhart's writings until I was overseas at university. He was a revelation and quite the discovery at the time. I hadn't come across anyone in the Christian tradition who was seeing things in a way similar to me. Eckhart came closest. It's remarkable, really, that his work survived. He certainly was not in my father's library. His influence is greater now than at any time since the 14th century. Incredible, isn't

---

27 John 1:3

it. I found his sermons not dissimilar to the traditional Indian teachings. He wrote about 'oneness,' saying that the knower and the known are one and the same.'[28] How courageous to say that God and creation are not two. You can see how inflammatory his findings would have been in those days."

"What about your mother? Could you talk to her about your findings?"

"My mother had converted to Christianity before she married my father, but never had much of an understanding of the gospel. If I had questions, I would often talk with her when my father was out. She was very sympathetic to my predicament and tried her best to listen."

"There wasn't anyone else you could talk to?"

"No one at all. I had only books and my own contemplations to go by."

"Would you say that it was the passage by Luke that began to open you up to a new understanding?"

"Not just Luke. At some point, I began to notice that, 'I am' was mentioned multiple times in the gospels. So I kept a notebook, which I called the book of 'I am's' and noted down all I could find. You know the main ones: "Be still and know that I am God,"[29] "I am the light of the world,"[30] "Before

---

28   *Meister Eckhart on Divine Knowledge*, C.F. Kelly.

29   Psalm 46:10.

30   John 8:12.

Abraham was born I am."[31] On my days off from school I would go into the surrounding mountains and contemplate, what this 'I am' might mean. Then, one sunny morning, while lying in the grass watching the vultures circling above me, I simply saw that I *was* this self-luminous 'I am.' Not the 'I' that points to a 'person' caught up in life. I saw the 'I' beyond the word. Aware-beingness that depends on 'no thing.' I was flooded with this presence and could hardly contain my joy. I wanted to go straight home and tell my father what I'd discovered."

"But you didn't?"

"No, of course not. Can you imagine the penalty if I had told him that the 'I am' referred to by Jesus was the very doorway to freedom? 'Father, guess what, I am the door.'[32] No, that would not have gone down well. To my father and everyone around him, Jesus was the door. If I had said that 'I am' is the key *and* the door, he would have heard that I was claiming Jesus was not the Son of God. Back then, I couldn't have explained that there is no door to 'all that is.'"

"As long as you're searching for the key there's a door to go through."

"Yes. The key is to stop searching and look at your actual experience."

---

31   John 8:58.

32   John 10:9.

"Did you think that this presence that you'd stumbled upon was separate in each person?"

"My understanding was immature and I hadn't looked at the consequences of discovering what I saw as the true 'I.' All I had was the certainty that I had seen something real; that there was *not* an individual residing here in this presence. Of course, now one wonders how it could have been missed."

"Did this presence stay with you after that morning or was there a sense that you had lost it?"

"No. It was gone by the time I reached home."

"So says thought!"

"Yes. So says thought. That was probably the day I became a serious seeker and, as you well know, there is nothing more difficult than seeking that which we already are."

"It's a bit like looking for your glasses when they're on your head."

"More like looking for your glasses when you looking through them."

"Had you been given any instruction in Hinduism?"

"When I was around seventeen, my mother decided that I should know something of Indian philosophy and religion. She encouraged me to spend time with the Hindu side of my family in Dehradun. It was there that my uncle first gave me books on Vedanta, the *Upanishads*, the *Ashtavakra Gita*, and many other works. When I went to visit him on weekends, I would plough through all the books he gave me. I was very excited with what I was reading and really loved to discuss the finer points of the sutras with him. Of course, I didn't dare take any of the books home."

"Did you continue reading the Christian doctrine after that?"

"Yes, at school I was still subjected to the gospel according to those around me, but it was different now. In the confines of my own home, I began to write down my own understanding of the teachings of Jesus. The Jesus I wrote about was more imaginative, more poetic than the Jesus of my religious instruction. What Jesus was saying to his disciples was not opposed to what the ancient Indian gurus stated, at least not in my interpretation. When Jesus said 'I am the truth, the way and the light,'[33] I understood him to be referring to this indivisible oneness."

"It's quite amazing that you never doubted yourself, considering the strong influences around you."

"I never once doubted what I had seen. I was completely on fire for truth and never once doubted what I now see as this simple indescribable presence. Jesus and many Indian sages made it unambiguously clear that the treasure of treasures is already always available and nothing could be more valuable or honest. I knew, and I had seen, that they were not lying. I had seen the kingdom and it was not the domain of the few. My only error at the time was that I thought there was a long

---

33   John 14:6.

and arduous path to it. And, like you Ray, I thought I needed to remove something to get to it."

"Did you seek out any Indian teachers at this time, Rudra?"

"You mean gurus. Yes, I did. My uncle introduced me to a few who spoke what appeared to be the truth. They had great charisma and told beautiful stories, but the experience of peace I found with them was short lived. One of the gurus of the time was your friend Tat Wale baba. Most impressive, I must say."

Rudra had mentioned that he knew of Tat Wale baba, but I hadn't realized that he'd actually met him.

"How long were you with Tat Wale baba?"

"I spent only one day up at his ashram, talking with him and exploring the caves and surrounding area. It was a beautiful and wild place back then."

"It's still lovely, Rudra but I'm sure you would see changes. Perhaps we could hike up there together sometime."

I poured us more tea without spilling a drop.

"Can you remember any of the questions that you asked Tat Wale?"

"Yes, I asked the same question to all the different teachers I met: 'Do you feel there is still more to be attained?'"

"How did Tat Wale answer?"

"He said exactly what I have been saying to you, but his expression was quite different. His responses sounded incredulous, as if saying, 'How could you possibly miss this!' I remember him looking straight at me and saying, 'You are omnipresent, omnipotent, and already fully attained.' Stirring words at the time. I was bold enough to ask him of his own attainment. Remember, at the time I thought there was something to seek out, to arrive at. He said something like, '"The mind was unaware of this. Now awareness is here. It is that simple.' Tat Wale was right. Why talk of attainment and further states beyond this splendor?"

Kasum appeared at the table, collected our tray, and left a jug of filtered water and two metal beakers for us.

Rudra poured us each a drink and then took a few sips.

"The meeting with Tat Wale was very helpful, but I didn't want to become a follower, so I moved on."

"You never really had a guru then?"

"Not formally, but I was exposed to many more gurus, teachers, and writers over the years."

"When did your own search come to an end? When did you come to this recognition?"

"Whenever I could, I hiked into the forest above our home with only one purpose: not to stop until I was free from the tyranny of the separate self. Or, as I understood the words of Jesus at the time, "when the eye is single and the body filled with light." I used to go and sit in the church near my home when it was raining and too wet to go into the forest. After many weeks I finally realized that trying to get rid of a separate self was like a knife trying to cut itself. Seeing that there was no *actual* separate entity was a huge realization. Struggling to get rid of a separate entity, when there isn't one, is quite a path to be stuck on, as you well know."

"Yes, I do."

"While I was sitting looking at the Himalayas one day, it dawned on me that the Father, the Son, and the Holy Ghost were not three. They were one. I saw that the Son and the Holy Ghost were expressions of the Father. I remember writing at the time that the Father was consciousness, the Son his self-reflection, and the Holy Ghost the primordial communion of love. Then I looked at the Hindu concept of *Sat Chit Ananda*—being, consciousness, bliss, and I saw that they were not three, they were one. From my point of view, the Father and the supreme non-dual reality Brahman had to be the same concept. Of course, when conceptualization ends, there is no doubt in its reality."

"Yes. What reality is more real than *this*?"

"Ray, you have perceived the sweetness of *this* and I'm overjoyed to see you recognizing yourself. Are you familiar with this quote from Saint Thomas? 'From me, all came forth, and to me, all attained. Split a piece of wood and I am there. Lift up a stone and you will find me there.'[34] Where am I not? Why would this self-luminous, aware-presence ever need enlightening?"

---

34 Gospel of Saint Thomas 77.

Rudra rose from the table and, turning around, I saw Dianne descending the steps from the kitchen carrying two *thali* trays. She was laughing and chatting with Kusum, who was walking behind her carrying another tray and a plate stacked high with *chapattis*.

"Hello Rudra. I hope you're both hungry. The *sabji* is pumpkin and we have *rajma* beans."

chapter eighteen

Queen of the Hills

Vijay, my taxi driver, dropped me off in Mussoorie in front of the old and dilapidated British cinema once known as "The Electric Picture Palace." Nothing was open yet and the snow added an eerie, deep quietness to the old shabby hill station. January is the best time of the year for clear views of the Himalayan range and, with a record low last night, the sky was sapphire blue and crystal clear. From the cinema, I had to walk two thousand feet higher, about an hour's trek, to reach Sister's Bazaar;[35] from there I would ask for directions to Rudra's house, where the caretaker was expecting me. It was bitter cold and, as I watched the old white Ambassador chug away, I pulled my

---

35 Sister's Bazaar was named after the British Raj-era dormitory building used by nurses.

woolen hat low over my ears and wrapped my scarf around my head and chin, Indian style. I was glad that Dianne convinced me to wear my thermal underwear.

My plan to walk to Rudra's house changed after only ten minutes, when a battered ambulance with "108" painted on the side[36] slowed down and its cheerful driver offered me a lift as far as the British Raj-era cantonment of Landour.

I opened the door to the strong smell of propane gas. "Emergency for hospital," he explained, tipping his head toward four large gas bottles wedged in the back of the van.

An hour from now, this single-lane road, originally a bridle path, would be bustling with honking taxis, vehicles full of schoolchildren, countless motorbikes, and pedestrians coming in all directions. The street, almost medieval in its decayed appearance, was hemmed in on both sides by crumbling three-story buildings and leaning power poles, tangled with hundreds of cables. Once, these properties were guesthouses and the ornate homes of merchants. Now they were occupied by cluttered cloth or electrical-parts shops and vegetable stalls.

The driver dropped me off just before the Community Hospital. From there, I made my way past the old British sanatorium to the long flight of steep stone steps leading up to Char Dukan.

---

36   This is the equivalent of our 911 for emergency services.

Noticing about twenty Nepalese men gathered on the roadside, I guessed from their threadbare clothes they were day laborers waiting to pick up some work. I signaled "namaste" to them and said "*Kasto cha*," which means "How are you," the only Nepalese I know. Tired faces lit up, one repeating "Kasto cha" back to me. I gave the greeting another try and they smiled and responded "*Thik cha.*" "Char Dukan?" I asked and they eagerly pointed chins and hands up the steps, some moving out of the way and shaking my hand as I passed.

A group of schoolchildren, dressed in thick blue blazers and gray trousers, bounded down the icy steps two at a time.

"Excuse me Uncle."

"Good morning Uncle!"

"How are you Uncle?"

"Good morning Uncle."

"Hello Uncle."

"Good morning Uncle!"

"Where are you going Uncle?"

"Hello Uncle!"

"Good morning," I shouted back as they slowed down, one at a time, to pass me. Scrubbed and spotless, the boys wore neatly combed side partings and the girls, red ribbons braided into long, shiny black hair. Giggling and jostling each other, the brave ones shook my hand.

"We are late you see Uncle."

"I'm fine thank you Uncle."

"Goodbye Uncle!"

The more-than-a-century-old Char Dukan, or "four shops," had increased to five small shops now, all in a neat row, protected from behind by enormous deodar trees. Crossing what was once a small parade ground for British soldiers, I headed straight to "Tip Top Cafe." Nearby, on higher ground, was another relic from the Raj: St. Paul's, a picturesque church erected in the 1830's and used as a garrison place of worship for British troops during the occupation.

The father-and-son proprietors greeted me, and I ordered my usual omelet sandwich, a special treat—no eggs in Rishikesh. Mr. Prakash senior was sitting in a spot of winter sun shining on the bench across from the shop. I joined him to bask and catch up on local news. Every time we met, he always reminded me, and anyone nearby, of my chat here with the great Sachin Tendulkar two years earlier. I had been sitting near Sachin eating breakfast. He was unrecognizable in his woolen hat and sunglasses. There were no other customers, so we began to chat—about the weather and about the spectacular scenery. I ordered more chai for both of us and we relaxed in the early morning sun. After Sachin left, Mr. Prakash senior sat down next to me and asked, "Don't you know who that is?" "No," I said, honestly, "but there was something familiar about him." When I told the ferry workers and the shopkeepers in Rishikesh that I had breakfast with Sachin Tendulkar, the most famous Indian cricketer in the world, it was as if I were Moses and had gone up the mountain and met God.

After breakfast, I climbed the icy steps to St. Paul's and sat quietly in one of the pews. The building smelled old and musty and of polish. I touched the carved-out notch and latch on the hymnbook ledge in front of me. How many homesick young soldiers, in full dress uniform, clamped their Enfield rifles into these holders before they knelt to pray?[37] The hymnbook in front of me was new, but the songs hadn't changed: "Abide with Me," "Holy, Holy, Holy," and, of course, "Jerusalem." I looked around to make sure the church was empty, then I held the book up to the light and sang William Blake's words aloud:

> And did those feet in ancient time
>
> Walk upon England's mountain green
>
> And was the holy Lamb of God
>
> On England's pleasant pastures seen

The hymn reminded me of dreary school assemblies during my youth in the British school system. I'd read that Blake hadn't written "Jerusalem" as a nationalistic battle cry for dominance and power, but as a vision of peace and democracy. The poem was based on a legend that Jesus came to England in his youth

---

37 After the Sepoy Rebellion in 1857, British soldiers in India were ordered
    to bear arms in church rather than stacking their weapons outside.

and established a second Jerusalem in the town of Glastonbury in Somerset.

Leaving the church behind, I walked along the tree-lined upper Chukkar loop and found myself reverting further into the British Raj era of the 1820s and 1830s. Thanks to an act established in 1924 banning any new construction or logging in this area, things hadn't changed much. The tigers and black bears, however, were not so lucky—the only evidence of their existence was mounted on hotel and guesthouse walls. The road was cut into the mountainside with huge retaining walls of rough-hewn stone decorated with vivid green moss and the mildewed streaks of old age.

Wrought iron gates and a driveway betrayed a lovely 19th-century white bungalow far below. I could see its high-pitched red roof, corrugated metal covered in patches of snow, and a large wraparound veranda and English style garden. No tire tracks on the road this morning, only a few footprints and paw marks in the snow. To my right, a driveway led upslope to a friend's house. He and his wife rent it year round and send their son to a private school here. Many of the old bungalows are summer homes with only a caretaker living in them during the cold season. The road curved and presented my first breathtaking view of the Garhwal Himalayas, towering above the valley and tiny villages below.

At Landour Cemetery, the dead were blanketed in snow, with little drifts pushing up against their headstones. The heavy bough of a deodar tree was lying over a now-horizontal stone cross, circa 1823. Dianne and I had wandered around this old British cemetery last year with the young daughter of the on-site caretaker. She knew the names of each cemetery resident and asked if we had a relative buried there. The headstones told of the hardship and suffering that the British occupiers endured for King and Country. Stories of husbands, wives, and children dying too young from dysentery, typhoid, cholera, and malaria. Men dying heroically in battle or falling down precipices with their horses and being dashed to pieces.

By the time I reached the confectionery shop in Sister's Bazaar, it was open. Mr. Prakash, in his late seventies and no doubt a relative of my friends at Tip Top, was behind the old wooden counter, where he had stood every day, as his father had before him, since British times. He was always threatening to retire, but here he still was. I hadn't seen him since last spring and was surprised when he recognized me. I ordered a hot cup of coffee and asked him to wrap up a hunk of his homemade "English" Cheddar cheese. We chatted as he cut the cheese from a huge round block that sat on the counter.

I couldn't imagine another shop remaining anywhere in India that represented the British Raj era like the Prakash Confectionary Shop in Sister's Bazaar did. The old wooden counter, glass display cases, enamel signs for Cadbury chocolate, Fry's, and Oxo were all original. The shop's dark, cluttered atmosphere would not have been out of place in a Charles Dickens story.

Warm from my hike, I sat outside in the sun. Mr. Prakash joined me, followed by his shop assistant carrying my coffee. He sat down, commenting, "I can't remember such a cold winter," and was about to continue when a huge brown monkey walked across the low wall opposite us. Mr. Prakash stood up, picked up a stone from his stash on the window ledge, and threw it, missing by a good four feet. He sat back down, having completely forgotten what he was going to say. Instead he told me how the monkeys have become a terrible menace.

"The local authorities have been catching them and shipping them off to the Rajaj National Park. Now Rishikesh is complaining that they are inundated with our monkeys. Delhi, too, has been trapping them and shipping them to the forests around Dehradun. The Langur's aren't a problem, but these brown ones are terrible pests. They are so aggressive."

I showed him the map that Rudra had drawn, indicating directions to his bungalow.

"Ah, you know Rudra?" he said. "His place is about a twenty minutes' walk from here. Just go straight along this road and you'll see his yellow mailbox and large white gateposts. You can't miss it. He's not there though. He's in Rishikesh now."

I told him that Rudra, a good friend, was letting me stay at his place for the night.

"Very good man. Very good man," he repeated, wobbling his head in an approving manner. "His family has owned that property for years."

He pointed to where Rudra had written "viewpoint" on the map.

"That's just behind his property. It might even be a part of the property. Best views in Mussoorie. Mind you don't get lost if you do go up there. It could be dangerous with all this snow"

I paid my bill, stuffed the cheese into my backpack, and told Mr. Prakash that I'd see him later.

I called out the caretaker's name as I opened the gate. Rudra's property was charming, and the old colonial bungalow, built in the 1840s with classic veranda and window shutters, was in excellent condition. A small brown-and-white dog ran full speed toward the gate, barking, stopping me in my tracks. The caretaker appeared and in English shouted at the dog to be quiet.

"Mr. Ray, sir." The dog relaxed, wagged its tail, lay down, and rolled over happily. Harish introduced himself as he brushed bits of wood and leaves from his hair and clothes. I noticed a big branch lying on the ground next to the house. Harish pointed to a tree and explained that the limb had broken off from a huge Himalayan oak during the night and crashed onto the roof, just missing a power line. It damaged the gutter as well as the roof, which he had already covered with a blue tarp held down with rocks. His wife walked across the garden with a bucket of snow balanced on her head. Harish introduced her as Vimala. She smiled brightly and tried to wobble her head as she said good morning.

Pointing to the bucket on her head, she said, "Pipes of water are frozen today." Harish explained that they had to melt snow for cooking and washing. As he helped lift the heavy container from her head, he asked, "Chai, sir?" With that, Vimala left to get it ready.

I took off my wet boots, entered the hallway, and found myself in a spacious sitting room with a vaulted ceiling and gleaming wood floor. The furniture was old fashioned and the room looked stiff and uninviting. It felt like a museum, displaying colonial tables and chairs, rattan rockers, chintz-covered settees with ornately woven cushions, and a beautiful Italian-looking chandelier. I studied several large framed black-and-white photographs: One showed a group of men standing at attention in formal attire, staring at the camera. Another showed men and woman dressed in white outfits holding tennis rackets. The women wore hats and long dresses to their ankles. I straightened a photograph of a man standing with his hands on his hips, legs apart, wearing a pith helmet. Also in the collection was a framed watercolor of a thatched-roofed English cottage surrounded by a lush flower garden, with the steeple of a church in the background.

I hadn't imagined Rudra living like a sadhu in a cave, but I would never have guessed that he lived in such colonial opulence. Harish appeared. "This room is never used," he said. "Please follow me."

"This is sir's study." He had already lit the gas fire in there, giving the room a warm, cozy feeling. The space was small and guarded by two grandly carved elephants flanking the entrance.

Double glass doors opened onto the veranda, where a couple of comfortable armchairs faced the garden. The end tables were piled with books and papers, and a computer, fax, and printer sat on a desk in the corner. On the bookshelf and sideboard were more framed photographs: Rudra's mother and father standing together in the garden; a smiling young girl and boy with the Himalayas behind them; Rudra and an attractive woman in a yellow sari with the same two children, only younger; Rudra and his father standing at the entrance to the London School of Economics.

Vimala entered with steaming hot chai and a plate of Marie biscuits.

Fifteen minutes later, there was a knock at the door. It was Harish.

"What time would you like lunch, sir?" I explained I wanted to hike this morning and would be back by two p.m.

Eager to get going while the skies were clear, I set off from the trailhead that Harish pointed out. Dianne and I had hiked here before but, with snow covering the path, it looked completely different. As I climbed higher, I followed the stonewall that originated close to the house. The steep incline eventually led me to a point that I recognized on Rudra's map. I veered east, plunged into the forest, winding through oak, fir, rhododendron, and deodar trees. Finally, I came into open space and could see a rocky outcrop ahead. I stopped to rest and marveled at the incredible windswept shapes in the snow between the trees. Rivulets of water from a steep slope to my left had glaciated mid-flow into stunning sculptures. Further up I saw a leopard's tracks the size of my palm. The marks were fresh and, thankfully, continued in the opposite direction.

I could see that I'd missed the viewpoint by about a hundred feet and had to wade through snowdrifts and brush to find it.

It was well worth the effort.

I stood on the large flat rock where Dianne and I had enjoyed many spring picnics and took in the glorious panorama. From this magical point, I could see the entire 125-mile Garhwal and Kumaon Himalayan range, the "Abode of the Gods." I identified the four Char Dham pilgrimage massifs of Yamnotri, Gangotri, Kedarnath, and Badrinath. To the east, I could make out the form of Nanda Devi and the peaks of Nepal. Tibet was only seventy miles straight in front of me.

I cleared a section of snow off the rock and sat down with my legs dangling over the edge. Below me was a vast drop into the valley. I took a deep breath. The air was pure and sharp as it entered my nostrils.

A fullness pervaded my entire being. No borders anywhere to be found. No separation between what I am and this present scene. This magnificence cannot be outside of me or other than me. This, of which I am aware, is this, which is aware. Who could be affected by the concerns of an apparent world? Nobody and no thing could be affected by anything. This endless mystery needs no explanation.

Since my talks with Rudra it is now impossible not to see, not to *be*, this ever-present foundation of peace and happiness. An equanimity that is not dependent on anything. Not even on a sense of being.

Krishnamurti had asked, "Are you not searching for something permanent? Some lasting certainty—because, in you, is uncertainty?" He was correct. I definitely was looking for a place to stand—a certainty free of uncertainty. A place where I was 'one' with all 'things.' For years, before I met Rudra, I believed that I had experienced this elusive oneness. I believed that the occurrence in Samantha's nightclub and Hyde Park was a foretaste of what I was looking for. During my time in Ojai with Krishnamurti, I believed that I had experienced oneness. There were also many glimpses of this 'oneness' on those long days practicing shakuhachi on that mountainside in Japan. I see clearly now that all those experiences were no other than appearances in this that already is, which is neither permanent nor impermanent. 'Permanent,' is of time and has its opposite in impermanent. Only from the point of view of thought could there be permanence or impermanence. Both are beliefs. There is only ever the real. As for a 'certainty,' what I am—is what this is. This is the certainty.

Cannot be grasped. Cannot be missed.

Here I sit in nature's most enduring environment, yet all I truly know of these famed Himalayan mountains is experience.

I closed my eyes—the mountains vanished. I turned my head and opened my eyes—perception again, now a snow-covered forest and then, back to the mountains. I cannot find an independently existing object or world. Nobody can. The discovery that 'objects' are not really 'objects' and that 'others' are not really 'others' is what we call love. The belief that there are objects and others separate from me is what we call suffering.

In the deep silence I suddenly heard a low growling noise coming from behind me. I braced myself for an attack and then, hearing a voice calling out, immediately relaxed. I turned around and saw an enormous black mountain dog glaring at me. He was wearing a weird, three-inch-wide tin collar around his throat and looked fierce. His owner, who was carrying a large bundle of wood on his head and a machete in his hand, yelled at the dog in the local dialect and the creature backed off. Relieved, I said namaste to the old man. He dropped his load to the ground and crouched down on his haunches. His wrinkled tanned face scrutinized me and then cracked into a red-toothed betel-nut grin. His eyes twinkled with warmth and laughter. He pulled out a packet of beedi cigarettes from his pocket and offered me one. I must have looked like an interesting 'perception,' worthy of a relaxing smoke. I refused his offer and watched him light up. I pointed to his dog's unusual collar and looked at the old man confused. "Baagh," he said, repeating the word and miming a man-sized cat holding its claws out. It was an anti-leopard collar.

For a few moments we looked across the valley and shared the majestic view. Perception dying in its beauty.

My visitor finished his beedi, heaved the bundle of wood back onto his head, and said goodbye.

Krishnamurti wrote, "No matter where you find yourself, no matter what background you come from, no matter what state of mind you're in, you can still look and see what is actually going on." Rudra reiterated the same message: "This is not for only a few 'special' beings. This is for anyone who has the earnestness and desire to look."

I began this journey believing that there was a distance between me and what I was longing for. I'd been told and I believed that someone or something needed to awaken. I'd been told and I believed that there was something to overcome. I was told and I believed that it would take tremendous effort to find peace, happiness, and freedom.

See for yourself that there is no one who could make such an effort. See that there is nothing to overcome. See that there is no one to be found who could possibly be troubled by anything. See that you were never bound, never *not* free.

Cannot be grasped. Cannot be missed.

glossary of sanskrit and hindi terms

Advaita . . . . 'not-two'; non-duality

Ayurvedic . . . . one of the oldest holistic healing systems

Baksheesh . . . . charitable gift, tip

Beedi . . . . Indian cigarette filled with tobacco
and wrapped in a leaf

Brahman . . . . the eternal imperishable absolute;
the supreme non-dual reality

Bhajan . . . . religious song of praise

Bodh Gaya . . . . . . Buddhist pilgrimage site in Bihar, India

Bhogi . . . . partaking in the material
world; without discipline

Bom Shankar . . . . sadhus shout this before inhaling
smoke from a *chillum* as a form
of worship to Lord Shiva

Chakra . . . . seven centres of spiritual power
in the human body

Charpoy . . . . simple bedstead surrounded
by a web of rope netting

Chillum . . . . conical pipe used for smoking hashish

Chalo . . . . let's go

Charas . . . . hashish

Dacoit . . . . bandit

Dhyana . . . . profound meditation practice of
Hinduism and Buddhism

Dupatta . . . . long scarf worn by women

Ganesh . . . . elephant god widely revered as the
remover of obstacles; patron of arts and
science; deva of intellect and wisdom

Guru . . . . spiritual teacher

Hari Om . . . . common greeting in Rishikesh;
mantra to remove suffering

Karma . . . . deed; consequences of mental
of physical action

Karah Prasad . . . . type of semolina made with whole-
wheat flour, butter and sugar

Kasto-cha. . . . . "How are you?" in Nepali

Khana. . . . . food; mealtime

Lassi . . . . blend of yogurt, water, spices
and sometimes fruit

Lungi. . . . . length of cotton material worn
by men around the body

Kurta . . . . loose collarless shirt worn by men

Mantra . . . . word or formula repeated to aid
concentration in meditation; a Vedic chant

Namaste. . . . . greeting; "I bow to the God within you"

Nani . . . . grandmother

Pagal. . . . . crazy

Panchakarma. . . . five-fold detoxification treatment
including massage, herbal therapy,
and other procedures

Paani. . . . . water

Patanjali . . . . sage who wrote the yoga sutras

Prasad . . . . food used as a religious offering
in Hinduism and Sikhism

Pūjā. . . . . act of making a spiritual connection with the "divine"; can be performed through invocation, prayer, song, and ritual

Raga . . . . Indian classical music

Ram . . . . Seventh Avatar of the Hindu God Vishnu

Rishikesh . . . . city in northern India; Valley of the Seers

Rudraksha. . . . . seed from the Rudraksha tree traditionally used for prayer beads in Hinduism

Saab . . . . equivalent to "sir"; term of respect

Sadhana. . . . . variety of spiritual disciplines in Hinduism and Buddhism

Sadhu . . . . wandering monk who has renounced the world

Samadhi. . . . . state that lies beyond waking, dreaming, and sleeping

Samskara . . . . imprints or impression left in the mind by experience

Sannyāsin. . . . . renunciant monk whose goal is liberation; initiated into and connected to an ashram

Sat Chit Ananda . epithet meaning "truth, consciousness, bliss"

Satsang. . . . . spiritual discourse or sacred gathering; in the company of the highest truth

Sattvic. . . . . eating in moderation food that is pure, essential, natural, energy containing, clean, conscious, and without meat, onions, or garlic

Shakuhachi. . . . . . Japanese bamboo flute

Shanti. . . . . inner peace

Shri . . . . venerable one

Siddhi. . . . . paranormal power

Sita . . . . consort of Ram

Savasana . . . . corpse pose in yoga

Thik Cha . . . . "I am fine" in Nepali

Thali . . . . round platter used to serve food

Turiya. . . . . pure consciousness

Upanishad. . . . . . . philosophical conclusion contained in the Vedas

Wallah . . . . worker; person in charge of a specific service or business

Vedas. . . . . sacred texts and hymns believed to have been written 2,500 years ago

bibliography

First and Last Freedom
J. Krishnamurti
Harper & Row,
ISBN 9780060648312

Freedom From the Know
J. Krishnamurti
Harpers San Francisco,
ISBN 9780060648084

You Are the World
J. Krishnamurti
ISBN 978-8187326021

*Wholeness and the
Implicate Order*
David Bohm
Routledge,
ISBN 0415289793

*Meister Eckhart on
Divine Knowledge*
C.F. Kelly
Frog books,
ISBN 1583942521

about the author and co-writer

Dianne and Ray Brooks - Tat Wale baba's cave

Ray Brooks, a writer, musician and recording artist, is internationally known in the world of shakuhachi music. He has studied with many great shakuhachi masters and performed throughout Japan and overseas. Born and raised in Newcastle-upon-Tyne, England, Ray at age sixteen moved to London.

Dianne Brooks, born in Oxford, England, is the co-writer of The Shadow that Seeks the Sun, and co-writer/creative editor of Blowing Zen: *Finding an Authentic Life.*

Sharing a passion for travel and adventure, Dianne and Ray have explored the world together, and continue to spend most of their winters in the foothills of the Indian Himalaya. They now live on Vancouver Island in Canada.

Contact: tststs@shaw.ca
Website: raybrooks.org

Blowing Zen
Finding an Authentic Life
Ray Brooks

In *Blowing Zen*, the author's reflections on his remarkable adventures in Japan are filled with insights as well as inspiration. This is the story of a modern-day *Komuso* (wandering monk), whose path to enlightenment is global in scope and whose drive to awaken is amplified only by the sound of the Zen bamboo flute, the shakuhachi.

—Monty H. Levenson

Reviews for Blowing Zen

"A genuine spiritual journey, finding Zen, music, and one's own true self. A lovely spirit blows through this book."

—Jack Kornfield, author of *A Path with Heart*

"Ray Brooks's unique and captivating book provides an insightful view of the heart and spirit of the Japanese culture and the musician's journey. In sharing his quest, he has enriched my life, and may inspire many others on the path of music, the ways of Zen."

—Dan Millman, author of *Way of the Peaceful Warrior* and *Everyday Enlightenment*

"A good book captivates—takes you to a different corner of the world and a different way of thinking. It's one you reach for again and again. *Blowing Zen* is such a book."

—Todd Shimoda, author of 365 Views of Mt. Fuji

"Not since Mickey Hart's *Drumming at the Edge of Magic* has a book so beautifully and eloquently exemplified the connection between spirit and music. *Blowing Zen* is a must-read for any musician or artist needing to manifest that connection."

—Greg Ellis, percussionist and co-founder of VAS